TRUTH AND EROS

FOUCAULT, LACAN, AND THE QUESTION OF ETHICS

JOHN RAJCHMAN

ROUTLEDGE NEW YORK AND LONDON

Published in 1991 by
Routledge
An imprint of Routledge, Chapman and Hall, Inc.
29 West 35 Street
New York, NY 10001

Published in Great Britain by
Routledge
11 New Fetter Lane
London EC4P 4EE

Cover art *Donna flagellata e baccante danzante,* Pompeii, Villa dei Misteri used by permission of Scala/Art Resource, New York.

Library of Congress Cataloging-in-Publication Data
Rajchman, John.
    Truth and eros : Foucault, Lacan, and the question of ethics /
John Rajchman.
        p.   cm.
    ISBN 0-415-90379-3.—ISBN 0-415-90380-7 (pbk.)
    1. Ethics, French. 2. Ethics, Modern—20th century. 3. Foucault,
Michel—Ethics. 4. Lacan, Jacques, 1901– —Ethics. I. Title.
BJ704.F68R34   1991
170'.92'244—dc20   91-7328
                                                                      CIP

British Library Cataloguing in Publication Data also available.

For Joel Fineman
In Memory and Friendship

Contents

Introduction

One of the great questions of ancient philosophy was: What is the eros of thinking? What is the eros of the peculiar sort of truth of which philosophy is the pursuit? What is the passion that drives one to philosophize, and that philosophizing requires of one? How does it come upon one, and when, and with what effects on oneself and one's relation with others? Doing philosophy was then thought to be a way of life, a whole game of mastery, rivalry and freedom in knowing, that had to defend itself against false pretenders. In these ancient agonistic "games of language," philosophers were to be *philoi*, friends; but friends of what and in what sense?

One cannot say that these are questions that play a very prominent role in contemporary English-speaking ethical philosophy. In our great debates over what is good for us and what is right for us to do, we have rather lost the sense in which to do philosophy *is* to entertain such passionate or erotic relations with ourselves and with others. And yet, we are today perhaps confronted with just this question: What can the passion of philosophy and of philosophical friendship still be in our civilization where scientific reason refuses all moral cosmology, and where socio-psychological expertise tries to replace all "charismatic" wisdom?

It is in order to rediscover such questions that I have turned to the work of two recent French thinkers, a psychoanalyst and a historian, Jacques Lacan and Michel Foucault. For I shall try to show that each of them in different ways tried to raise again the ancient question of truth and eros; each of them in different ways re-eroticized the activity of philosophical or critical thought for our times. Together, they thus helped to create an intellectual climate that was to capture the imagination of a generation, and with which we are perhaps not yet done. One aim of this book is to try to get at the *ethos* of this new passion for philosophy or critical thought, which has incited in some fears of a corrosive nihilism and a cynical inactivity.

In particular, I will argue that by degrees, the question of truth and eros involved these two thinkers in a long and involuted reflection on ethics; and that, conversely, if the question of ethics in their work is of a peculiar or unfamiliar sort, it is because of the ways it is inseparable from the ancient question of the passion of thought. By way of introduction I start with the problem of the difficulty of their *styles* of thought or philosophy.

Lacan and Foucault were formed by the different "generations" of the twenty-odd years that separate them. They held different and often opposing views. It is not sure whether they were friends or foes, for they wrote little about one another. And yet at the outset, we may observe that their attempts to rethink eros, and to re-eroticize thought, were ones fraught with great difficulty; and that this difficulty was at the heart of their efforts to invent new styles of thought.

What is a philosophical difficulty, the sort of difficulty that provokes one to philosophy and that philosophy is designed to treat? And why, in the case of these two thinkers, does this sort of difficulty become more insistent or tangible the more closely one approaches the question of ethics in their work? Or, put the other way around, why is the style of each, as a style of ethical thought, such a difficult one? Neither figure was an author of what might be thought to be the traditional ethical forms. They did not write novels, deliver sermons or pronounce prophecies. They did not write Confessions or Meditations or Manifestoes; they left no ethical "treatise" and proposed no "groundwork" for the metaphysics of moral codes. Why is it that the discussion of ethics is rather scattered throughout their work, and linked to many other preoccupations?

As is the case for all great philosophy, the works of Lacan and Foucault were difficult ones, conceptually, rhetorically and thematically. And yet their difficulties were of a rather more peculiar and specific sort. The difficulty of Lacan's work at least was in part by design. He prided himself on having written what others must initially find unreadable. In 1957 he declared: "I like to leave the reader no other way out than the way in, which I prefer to be difficult";[1] and many who thus found their way in never came out. He wanted to jolt or surprise with the words he used, and could be quite blunt. At the same time he cultivated a singular style he himself called "Gongoristic" and "Baroque"—hermetic, highly literate, replete with sophisticated jokes and puns, arcane allusions, neologisms and strange formulae and graphs to which he himself gave different readings as he went along. And yet Lacan's difficulty was as much necessity as affectation: he thought he *could* write or speak in no other way and say what he thought he had to say. He was someone who wrote and spoke *out of* difficulty.

This style inevitably attracted charges of obscurantism, charlatanism, and intellectualism. Foucault did not see it that way. He said people came to Lacan for the mere pleasure of reading or listening to a discourse without visible institutional support; and if what they heard or read was difficult, it was because it was intended that they should "realize themselves" in reading or listening to it.

It is significant that among those who would have thus come to Lacan, philosophers, those trained in philosophy in France, played a prominent part. Lacan's style may have been difficult, but through it was created a whole alliance of psychoanalysis not just with the history of philosophy, but also with epistemology, logic and the history of science. Part of the drama and the difficulty of Foucault's last work would lie in its attempt to depart from the singular importance psychoanalysis had acquired in contemporary French philosophy, largely through the work of Lacan.

The difficulty of Foucault's own work is of a different sort. He wrote in a much more classical style, less extravagant, more synoptic and demonstrative, and in this sense, argumentative and more combative. In contrast to Lacan, it was a style to create single self-contained books, of which *Discipline and Punish* would be the most realized example—a work Foucault would later call "my first book."[2]

And yet in his last writings, where he sought to depart from psychoanalysis, and where the question of ethics is most insistently posed, Foucault tried to abandon this style, with its powerful philosophical and conceptual armature. He thus found himself with a difficulty in which he tried to rethink what a style, and thus what *his* style in philosophy, was.

In both cases we may then say that the difficulty with which their work confronts us corresponds to a difficulty they experienced in creating it, a difficulty that recurs in the reflection of each on the style of his own thought, its means, its aims, its relations with institutions. The question of their style was thus a question of who they saw themselves as being in relation to their work, and that is how it came to be linked to the ethics, and to the eros of their thought.

Accordingly, I will now look more closely at their difficulties and their styles, trying to trace how they come to involve ethics. In the following chapters I will then reverse directions, and starting from the questioning of ethics in the work of each thinker, show in what ways it led to an attempt to devise a new style or a new passion of thought for our times.

Foucault's Freeing of Himself

In his last writings Foucault tried to "disengage himself" from the style of his previous books, and the kind of "philosophical experience" in which that style had been rooted, or which it had served:

> Very abruptly, in 1975–76, I completely gave up this style, for I had it in mind to do a history of the subject, which is not that of an event that would be produced one day and of which it would be necessary to recount the genesis and the outcome.[3]

This abrupt "refusal" of his earlier style marked a shift in the basic questions of his historical research. The "question of the subject," and therefore of "individual conduct" came to the fore. Foucault declared that this question could not, and so should not, be separated from those of his earlier work, and of "himself" in that work—namely the questions of truth and of power. He thus tried to invent "other rhetorical methods" that would not avoid "the question of the subject" in addressing these other two.

At the same time, this search for a style that would not avoid "the question of the subject" provided Foucault with the occasion to raise in a new way the central philosophical question that had run throughout his work: What is thought (*pensée*)? What is its singular entangled history, and what are its unrecognized critical possibilities? In 1975–76, he started to ask: What does thought have to do with subjectivity, or with the "question of the subject"? In particular, in which ways can it be said that "thought" forms part of a "way of life"? What role has it played, and might it yet play, in the manner in which one leads or conducts one's living? That is how Foucault's search for a new style in his last writings led him back to the ancient problem of philosophical ethics, and, more specifically, to the question of the *eros* of thought in the conduct of one's life. For it was through a history of sexuality reaching back to the Greeks that the question of his style would be raised.

The period of this search and research was a time of difficulty. It was a time of shifting alliances and friendships, and of many travels. Foucault thought he might take a break from his archival research and try his hand at journalism. He spent time in a Zen monastery in Japan. He went so far as to consider taking up residence in Berkeley, California. Gilles Deleuze speaks of Foucault as having gone "through a crisis of all orders, political, vital, philosophical"; adding that "the logic of a thought (*pensée*) is the set of crises it goes through."[4]

The way in which Foucault elaborated his style of thought seems to follow this Deleuzian principle. First there was the famous crisis in "Man" as a basic founding entity, through which Foucault argued it had become possible to think again. The anonymity with which this new question was thus "posing itself" in our thought led Foucault to invent a style that would refuse the individualizing "face" of traditional authorship. Then there was a crisis in the political assumptions of an ambient "textualism," and the discovery of thought as a form of strategic combat. It led to a style of writing as an act of resistance or revolt. "All my books are tool-boxes," Foucault declared. Yet a few years later he would say that his books were "fragments of an autobiography." There was then a third crisis, Foucault's difficulty with himself as anonymous historian and militant. It raised the question of what the activity of critical thought means for the experience of those engaged in it. The problem of style in writing became a problem of style in living.

Style was thus a matter of "How I wrote certain of my Books," and belonged to a long tradition in which that sort of problem had been raised. Raymond Roussel may be thought to be the very example of a writer obsessed with language and not "the world." But in a late interview about this writer for whom he kept a special affinity, Foucault declared that Roussel's work was important for his life, not because he expressed or represented himself in it, but because of the singular way in which it formed part of the way he had conducted it. The same would be true for Foucault: writing books would not be a way of expressing himself, but would form part of a way of living. In his case at least, each book would be an attempt to get away from the experience of the previous ones and to make a new start: "To write a book is in a certain way to abolish the preceding one."[5]

In introducing his last histories, Foucault says that this subjective experience of making books is normally kept "off-stage," *dans les coulisses*, as one presents one's book as a finished product to the public. One might say that this was a precept Foucault himself had adopted in his writing in the agon of revolt, and the anonymity of the question. But in his search for a style that would not avoid the question of the subject, he tried to bring out the sense in which, for him, to write a book was an experience and an exercise in thought:

> It would probably not be worth the trouble of making books if they failed to teach the author something he hadn't known before, if they didn't lead to unforeseen places, if they didn't disperse one toward a strange new relation with himself. The pain and pleasure of the book is to be an experience.[6]

From 1961 to 1969, Foucault had published six books. By contrast, from 1976 to 1985, during his "difficulty," he published no books, except those which, were it not for his dying, he would probably not have published. He envisaged several books he never completed, and told of the many uncertainties surrounding those he did. What remains from the "crisis years" is rather an unwieldy mass of courses, reviews, interviews, lectures, and pieces of journalism, concerning a wide variety of topics and questions, given on various occasions, linked to different groups within academia and without. It is difficult to grasp as a whole. His search for "other rhetorical methods" that would not avoid the question of the subject remained unfinished, the difficulty of his new style, unresolved. It is rather the *search* for a style that his last writings exemplify, something as when it is said that what was important about Socrates was his pursuit of the good, rather than his discovery of it.

The difficulty of Foucault's last writings is a puzzle his work leaves us. This "writing in difficulty" of the last decade of his life remains at once the most intimate and the most free part of his work—the one people have known the least what to make of, or what to do with, the part that is the least classifiable, the most up for grabs.

There are of course those who don't want to see Foucault's difficulty, or to see Foucault in difficulty, people who wish he had kept his difficulty to himself, private, "off-stage." There are people who believe that tool-boxes oughtn't to be confused with autobiographies, and that Foucault's problems with himself should be distinguished from his contributions as a critical intellectual and historian. They wish that Foucault had stuck with his earlier style of philosophy that avoided the question of the subject, and that, in taking it up, he had forfeited the achievements of his studied anonymity. There are, in short, those who find Foucault's last "concern with himself" a self-centered, individualistic, and therefore asocial or apolitical one. We might imagine Foucault responding to such objections in the following manner.

In the first place, to have a "concern for oneself" has been a distinctive mark and a basic difficulty of critical or philosophical thought since Socrates—part of what it is to be a philosopher. "This critical function of philosophy, up to a certain point, emerges right from the Socratic imperative: 'Be concerned with yourself, i.e. ground yourself in liberty, through mastery of self.' "[7] To think critically or philosophically *is* thus to be concerned with oneself; the difficulty is to know *how*. More strongly, "subjectivity" *belongs* to critical thought; it cannot be avoided.

Secondly, the view that such a concern is something that one must try to eliminate or keep to oneself is a late development, whose assumptions merit examination. Through a long history, the ancient preoccupation with the self was turned into a matter of vanity, pride, self-interest or self-love, the very opposite of "selfless" or charitable relations with others, or a private obstacle to the realization of a rational, public or collective good. A Christian tradition had taught that self-renunciation is the means to salvation. A secular tradition had tried to base morality in a public law, external to the self. And finally, with the scientific discovery that Nature was external and amoral, a philosophical tradition "from Descartes to Husserl" tried to shift the critical concern for the self onto the "knowing" or epistemological subject. It had tried to "superimpose the functions of spirituality on an ideal based in scientificity."[8] Two interconnected results would follow from these profound developments in "the subjectivity" of critical thought. The first is that "our morality, a morality of asceticism, insists that the self is that which one can reject"; the second is that "knowing oneself" has obscured and replaced the ancient task of taking care of, or being concerned with, oneself.[9]

It is then these views that had linked asceticism with the ideal of a transcendent reason modelled on law, science or theology, from which Foucault sought to depart in his attempt to restore the Socratic principle that to do critical philosophy is to be concerned with oneself. His difficulty was correspondingly to invent an *askēsis*, a "subjectivizing" practice of critical thought, where the relation to oneself is not rooted in the idea that the self is what we can reject, and where the aim is not the submission to an external law, independent of our experience of ourselves.

There is then a third point. There is a sense—one might say a Wittgensteinian sense—in which Foucault's "difficulty" *could* not be a private one. For, in arguing that subjectivity cannot be avoided in critical thought, Foucault was not attempting to return to a pre-critical or pre-philosophical experience of a founding subject everywhere the same. On the contrary, he held that "subjectivity" is constituted through various and changing public practices. Our subjectivity is not given by an intrinsic nature, theological, theoretical, or natural. There is no one single form of it, and Foucault thought the attempt to discover such a form, applicable to all, had had disastrous results.

In this Foucault continues a precept of his earlier research; for there is nothing private about the inherited use of words and practical techniques Foucault had set out to analyze in his histories of madness, crime or disease. On the contrary, he sought to expose the cunning or ruse of self-identification or self-knowledge in making our subjective experience *seem* private, natural or absolute. That is why one may say, as with Wittgenstein, that for Foucault, "subjective" experience is never absolutely private. Unlike Wittgenstein, however, Foucault adopted the hypothesis that the question of the subject cannot be separated from the questions of knowledge and of power. His subjective difficulty with himself as historian and militant was tied up with the question of the relation of his critical thought to the kinds of scientific knowledge we accept about ourselves, and the forms of government and self-government with which they are linked.

Foucault's concern with himself was thus not a matter of an ascetic escape from earthly power and knowledge to another "truer" realm. It rather raised the question of what form the experience of free critical thought should assume when confronted with our ways of knowing and governing ourselves. Foucault's difficulty was then not private in a further sense; the problem it defined was not a problem for him alone.

One consequence of Foucault's historical, public conception of subjective experience is that our "subjectivity" is not the same as our "individuality"; a person is not confined by logic or nature to his identifications of himself. For there arise moments when people cease to accept the practices that define them, moments of "difficulty" in our historical constitution of ourselves. It was just in such moments that Foucault thought people had a particular kind of experience of critical thinking. For this reason, he presented his own difficulty with himself as intellectual and historian as part of a more general crisis or difficulty in the "function" of the intellectual and the historian, connected with the experience of a failure in progressive utopian ideals. His difficulty would then be part of *our* difficulty as critical thinkers or philosophers.

Foucault's search for a style that would not avoid the question of the subject was, in short, a search for an experience and a practice of critical thought that would not be separated from the forms of knowledge and power we accept, and which would not be based in the "ascetic" assumption that the subject is something we can reject in the name of an ideal of rationality. What would it mean to be freely concerned with ourselves when it is not a matter of sacrificing the part of ourselves that stands in the way of our discovery of a higher truer nature? What would it mean to speak truly and critically about ourselves, without the assurance of being able to know in advance the invariant principles or rules that would apply to the living of each and all of us? One can say at least this: the *eros* of this experience of critical thought would not be a sacrificial or renunciatory one; it would not be perfectionist, salvationist or progressivist; and it would not assume the form of inducing people to accept principles or rules known independently of their experience of themselves.

It is not entirely fortuitous that Foucault's search for a new style in the subjectivity of critical thought coincided with his research into the history of what we call our "sexuality." For sexual, passionate, erotic experience is a domain in which the refusal of asceticism has been particularly pronounced. It is here that the finger of suspicion about asceticism has been especially pointed, its illnesses most diagnosed, the social and political consequences surrounding it most clear. And, in all of this, of course, Freud has played a central part.

But Foucault thought it was not enough to expose the discontents of our erotic asceticism. He wanted to at least raise the question of another and non-ascetic way of making our erotic "subjectivity," another sort of philosophical *askēsis*. He asked what role friendship among men, old and young, should play in this *askēsis*, when traditional definitions and practices had become problematic, and where what a "friendship" is became open and undefined.

"Asceticism as the renunciation of pleasure has bad connotations. But the *askēsis* is something else. . . . Can that be our problem today? We've rid ourselves of asceticism. Yet it is up to us to advance into a homosexual *askēsis* that would make us work on ourselves and invent, I do not say discover, a manner of being that is still improbable."[10]

In short, Foucault's difficulty in his passionate, affective relations as in his experience of making books, was to invent a new non-ascetic eros in the exercise of critical thought.

In his last work, and his last conception of his work, Foucault formulated this difficulty in terms of the question: What does it cost for reason to tell the truth? With this question he reformulated an earlier category of the experience of his critical practice: the category of the intolerable. *L'intolérable* was the title of a publication Foucault helped to establish that demanded to know, and to make known, "what the prison is." It said there arise occasions when people will no longer tolerate their conditions, without possessing in advance a procedure or theory to know what to do about it. They thus demand "information" about this condition, not simply from officials, but, in this case, from anyone "who, in one capacity or another, has an experience of the prison, or a relation to it."[11] The role of the "specific intellectual" is not to supply officials with a policy to resolve the difficulties in this complex and anonymous experience, but rather to analyze the costs of everyone's participation in maintaining it. The example of such a "specific" exercise in critical thought would be *Discipline and Punish*.

Foucault then conceived "the intolerable" in terms of the theme of the costs of our own self-constitution. In his last writings, he often declares that we know ourselves, we govern ourselves, and we make ourselves only at a cost, which we often pay without recognizing, or without realizing that is not necessary to do so. One task for "critical thought" is thus to expose these costs, to analyze what we did not realize we had to say and to do to ourselves in order to be who we are. That, at any rate, would have been what Foucault himself had been trying to do.

> How does it happen that the human subject makes himself into an object of possible knowledge, through which forms of rationality, through which historical necessities, and at what price? My question is this: How much does it cost the subject to be able to tell the truth about itself? How much does it cost the subject as a madman to be able to tell the truth about itself? . . . A complex and multi-layered totality with an institutionalized frame, class relationships, class conflicts, modalities of knowledge, and finally a whole history . . . That is what I tried to reconstitute. . . . And I want to continue that in respect to sexuality. How can the subject tell the truth about itself as a subject of sexual gratification, and at what cost?[12]

The experience of critical thought would start in the experience of such costs. Thus, before asking, or at least when asking, what we must do to behave rationally, this kind of thinking would ask: What are the "forms of rationality" that secure our identity and delimit our possibilities? It would ask what is "intolerable" about such forms of reason; "how much does it cost Reason to tell the truth?"

This sort of critical experience would then confront us with a different sort of difficulty, and with a different relation to our difficulties than the "ascetic" one that asks us to reject ourselves in order to behave properly or rationally. Foucault puts the difference in a passage that refers to Max Weber.

> It is a question of the relation between asceticism and truth. Max Weber posed the question: if one wants to behave rationally and regulate one's action according to true principles, what part of one's self should one renounce? What is the ascetic price of reason? To what kind of asceticism should one submit? I posed the opposite question. How have certain kinds of interdiction required the price of certain kinds of knowledge about oneself? What must one know about oneself in order to be willing to renounce anything?[13]

Asceticism tried to determine what we must sacrifice of ourselves to know what is good or right; it had sought to define the "legitimate" violence, the pain and the pleasures, of turning ourselves into beings of the right sort, virtuous or dutiful. Foucault would start instead with a different sort of violence—the violence of our own historical self-constitution. Our freedom would lie in our recognition that this violence is not a necessary one, that it is subject to reversal and transformation; it is a violence we can identify, we can cease to accept, and in whose workings we can refuse to participate. To recognize it, to seek to reverse it, is also a violence of sorts. But this violence in our capacities for critical reflection and action is not in itself ascetic: it does not suppose that we know in advance who we should be; it does not follow from it that we must renounce ourselves. It instigates another kind of critical reflection about ourselves and our possibilities, that asks whether we are still willing to *tolerate* the violence we do to ourselves, to know, to govern, and to make ourselves.

> Maybe the target nowadays is not to discover who we are but to refuse who we are, . . . we have to promote new forms of subjectivity through the refusal of this kind of individuality that has been imposed on us for several centuries.[14]

But this refusal of our "individuality" is not an attempt to ascend to another purer world, a philosophical republic, but to experience something not yet done or thought in *this* world. It is the experience of a critical "transcendence" without a "transcendental" ideal, regulative or constitutive. It is not a requirement of Eternity, but a concrete problem of history. That is why Foucault's *déprise de soi* would not be an ascetic "detachment" from life, but the start of a new way of living.

Foucault thus defined a particular kind of difficulty in thought: the difficulty of those moments when we cease to tolerate our conditions, banding together in critical action and reflection; the moments when our self-identifications seem contingent and violent in ways we hadn't realized; the moments that separate us from our "individualities," exposing their costs and raising the open question of their refusal. The subjectivizing experience of critical thought would arise from these moments, when it is no longer a matter of "discovering" ourselves, but of "crossing the line" to a new and improbable identity.

It is then that philosophical friendship becomes a "friendship in difficulty." If the Platonic eros was a matter of the *philia* of those who turn around the eyes of their souls to the timeless *sophia* they had forgotten, this would be the *philia* of those who experience the contingency of their historical being, and expose themselves to the unchartered *sophia* of a "strange and new relation" to themselves.

Foucault's "crisis" in his last work was thus not a personal crisis in his ideals. He was not asking: What are the intrinsic values I have offended, and which I am now prepared to advance and exemplify, and so attain wisdom or guidance in my actions? His "philosophical exercise," his "ascesis," his "experimentation" with himself in his work would not, in the manner of the "spiritual autobiography" of Augustine, assume the form of an exemplary conversion. On the contrary "*se déprendre de soi-même* is the opposite of a conversion."[15] Unlike the "confessions" of Rousseau, it would not entail a search for a pre-social or natural identity or self-relation. On the contrary, it would be based on the idea that "the subject is not given." Unlike the "meditations" of Descartes it would not be a search for certainty or "evidence" in thought or action. On the contrary, it would question the evidence on which our thought and our action rest. Unlike Freud's *Interpretation of Dreams*, it would not be the search for a constitutive *desire*; in contrast to Sartre, it would not be a search for a basic *choice*.

Foucault did not see the difficulty in his last work as a spiritual, a sceptical, a moral or a psychological crisis. The source of his ethical difficulty would not be a moral fault, a methodological doubt, a bad faith, or a neurosis. And his response to it did not assume the form of an act of repentance, an overcoming of uncertainty, an auto-critique, or a psychotherapy. It would not have the "ascetic" form of: How have I strayed from God or Reason (and so from myself), and how can I repent and rediscover myself?; or How in sorting out which of my thoughts are dubitable can I arrive at the certainty of a method?; or How can I find again who I really am beyond all the social alienations to which I have been submitted? It was not a practice of "remembering" where he had gone astray, but of an *anamnesis* of what he had been unable to see in what he had been doing and thinking. He thought of his crisis as a crisis in the limits of the work of which he was capable.

What Foucault came to admire in Lacan was this difficulty he had found in his own search for a new style. It was in these terms that, writing at the time of his death, Foucault paid this homage to the psychoanalyst:

> It seems to me that what makes for the whole interest and force of the analyses of Lacan is precisely this: that Lacan was the first since Freud to want to recenter the question of pscyhoanalysis on the problem of the relations between the subject and truth. . . . He tried to pose the question, which is historically a "spiritual" question: that of the cost the subject has to pay in order to say the true, and that of the effect on the subject of the fact that he can say the true about himself.[16]

In psychoanalysis, Lacan would have found a new way of formulating the "spiritual" question of *dire-vrai* about our sex, or our eros. He would have formulated it for a time dominated by market, bureaucracy and science, in which the older cosmological, holistic communitarian identifications had eroded and lost their hold. He was the orator who brought this eros, and its difficulties, into the medicine of sex and the practice of philosophy.

Lacan as a Self-Made Man

Lacan was a great orator. He spurned what he called *poubellication*— casting his thought in the publishing trash can. What he published was mostly what he had already said. His thesis from the thirties, published in seventies, is his only real book. What are called his *écrits* comprise pronouncements on occasions, condensations of his Seminar, rococo proposals, reviews, peculiar institutional documents and addresses. The central vehicle of his thought was not a written form at all. It was his thirty-year long Seminar, the most constant institution in his stormy institutional career, which, only late in his career, did he undertake to have transcribed and published. And yet in one such Seminar, *Encore* of 1972, Lacan confides that there was one book he would have liked to prepare for publication. Its topic would be ethics. It is as if Lacan dreamt of a great book on ethics he could never bring himself to publish, of which his Seminar would have been a vast preparation and exemplification. Lacan was thus like the master of an ancient ethical School, such as Stoicism or Cynicism, who leaves behind disciples, an entangled *Nachlass* and many anecdotes of a history.

We might understand the "difficulty" of Lacan's style—the difficulty he had with it, and the difficulty he intended it to make for others— in this context of an orator who becomes the master of a School. Lacan was proud to say he had no "worldview," no *Weltanschaung*. In its place he would have a style. "*Le style c'est l'homme même,*" he wrote by way of introducing his *Ecrits* published in 1966 (the same year as Foucault's *Les Mots et les Choses*), giving the seventeenth century motto a new interpretation for a period where "Man" was no longer so certain a reference. Perhaps, to "rally" people, it should now, or in his case, be thought to refer to "the man" to whom the style was addressed—this Other. And this style, in the absence of a worldview, addressed to a now uncertain "man," was to form part of what he came to call his "teaching" (*mon enseignement*), and it would lead, a few years later, to the founding of a "Freudian School," *une école freudienne*.

It is through this style of a "teaching" that Lacan gave a new erotic impetus to the activity of thought in France. He declared that in offering people the possibility of speaking about themselves in a certain manner, he had created a great demand (unlike the market mechanism where it is the demand that creates the supply, or *offre*). While he wrote not a single case study, he thus offered more than one generation a novel and concrete picture of what it is to conduct an analysis. He helped to invent a philosophico-literary avant-garde, a "culture of the letter," that flourished in the sixties, and was later to become important in the American university. He introduced psychoanalysis into the epistemo-logical question of what a science is and can be. He was someone who brought to psychoanalysis a greater philosophical culture, and perhaps also a more insistent philosophical desire, than is found in Freud.

The history of Lacan's Seminar is the history of its displacement through the clinical, academic and public institutions of Paris. Around it crystallized a new and increasingly diverse sort of public: the mostly clinical one at the Hospital of Sainte Anne, the young Althhusserian one at the Ecole Normale Supérieure, and the large disparate one at the Panthéon. But the "school" that thus came to form around this orator was not part of, and was not modelled on, the university or the professional medical association. It conferred no diplomas, required no thesis or maîtrise, had no curriculum or "canon," and didn't define itself in relation to other "faculties." On the contrary, Lacan claimed for it an "extraterritorial" status; in it would reign a different sort of "mastery" than that of university discourse, or technocratic qualifica-tion. Lacan's seminar had taken up again the risk and the drama of a public oration where the one who speaks is recognized or authorized by his own relation to the truth, his own activity of analysis.

For Lacan's Seminar was not only a place for the formation of analysts, it was also the place of his own self-formation. It was a place of his dreams; he invested himself in it, he lived and died in it and through it. It was the public space of his singular *ethos*, of the necessity that compelled him to continue *encore*. The Seminar was "that thanks to which what I teach is not self-analysis," he declared in an appearance on television in which he says, using the English expression, that he is a "self-made man."[17]

The principle underlying Lacan's "difficulty" was not to separate this pedagogical, formative and self-formative *eros* from what it taught, but to reintroduce the question of what it taught into the manner in which it was transmitted. The difficulty of his style would in this sense be the difficulty of what it is to acquire and to impart a knowledge of the unconscious.

In her history of French psychoanalysis, Elizabeth Roudinesco ex-plains that Lacan's Seminar had a philosophical model or precursor:

the Seminar of Alexandre Kojève that was to have a varied and seminal influence on post-war French philosophy. And of course Kojève was also someone who found it difficult to write, but who influenced many who did not. But one might also mention another more ancient philosophical master, who had notorious difficulties with writing—the one whose dictum was "impiety is ignorance." For as with Socrates, the difficulty of Lacan's teaching was a difficulty in what it is to speak truly of oneself; it was the difficulty of an *ethics*.

But if Lacan's style was, in these respects, like the orational style of an ancient master in ethics, it was designed for a modern time much altered in its basic assumptions—a time when the "man" to which it was addressed was no longer so certain a reference, or which denied the possibility of a worldview. What is "modern" about Lacan's difficulty, or what would distinguish the teaching of the unconscious from the teachings of ancient wisdom, would lie in its principled refusal of any supposition of a knowledge of the Good, or of any Ideal we might imitate in virtue. Its ethic would rather be an ethic or teaching of the difficulties we have with what is ideal in us, and with what we suppose is our Good, and thus with our passionate relations with ourselves and one another. That is why it requires another sort of passion than the one that follows from the supposition of a Good or an Ideal, and the relations of rivalry, mastery and identification such a supposition would carry with it. It requires another eros and another conception of eros for a time marked by the ideologies of Science and Free Enterprise, which deny us the possibility of finding our eros in the general goodness of the world. The difficulty would be how to be "friends" in this modern world. It was Lacan's view that Freud showed us how. The innovation of Freud was to have supplied and set to work a new kind of eros in our knowing or speaking truly about ourselves: "Psychoanalytic discourse has a promise: to introduce something new. This, *chose énorme*, in the field in which the unconscious produces itself, since its impasses, among others of course, but in the first place, are revealed in love."[18]

It is the kind of eros we would experience in the *place* of wanting to know about ourselves, the eros of the difficulty we experience in relation to the good or the ideal. In introducing this eros in his teaching, Lacan's school would thus be a "Freudian School." "Psychoanalysis is not an idealism," Lacan would never stop saying; it is not an ethic of the good. "My aim," he would declare, "is to extract ethics from *Bien-dire.*"[19]

It would seem that Lacan developed this picture of a new Freudian ethic in the thirties, when fascism was on the rise in Europe. Between his early work as a young psychiatrist in the thirties, before his style would assume its difficult "Baroque" forms, and the institution of his Seminar in the fifties, the War intervened. The War was something of a "traumatic event" in more ways than one. Its effects on psychoanalysis were dramatic; it served to transport Freud and the center of psychoanalysis from central Europe to Britain and the United States. In particular, it brought with it Lacan's own short war-time analysis with Lowenstein, en route to America, where he helped start the "ego-psychology" Lacan would see as a betrayal of psychoanalysis. But the war may also be said to have had another effect: to have confirmed in Lacan his inveterate hatred or horror of "idealism," and thus of an ethic of the good.

Lacan's early writings were focused on the theme of agressivity, crimes of passion and the peculiarities of the eroticism of mad women. Retrospectively at least, we may note how they provided a theoretical underpinning of this horror of idealism.

In his analysis of the "erotomania" of the woman he called Aimée, and later in his famous paper on the mirror phase, Lacan advanced the view that our relation to what is "ideal" in us, to our ideal-egos as well as our ego-ideals, derives from a fundamental violence or "alienation," shown in the clinical imagery of *le corps morcelé*. At bottom the ego *is* a self-"idealization" required to enter the social order; and that is why our identity is inherently violent, involving us in the "imaginary passion."

If psychoanalysis is not an idealism, it is because it proposed a treatment whose principle is to refuse to enter into this imaginary passion. For what is new or distinctive about psychoanalysis is that it bases its treatment on another conception of the being of the doctor and the patient than that of what is ideal in one or the other, and on the passion that follows from it. Psychoanalysis would be a treatment that does not propose an "ideal" for the self, but concerns itself with the inherent agressivity in our relation to such self-images.

It thus introduces a peculiar ethical difficulty: it can no longer base itself in the idealizing view of love or friendship as they have been traditionally understood. The passion that binds doctor and patient in the difficult work of analysis is unlike that of the ancient philosophical *philoi*, and unlike that of Christian neighbors. Analysis is neither eros nor agape; it is not wisdom or altruism, and an analyst is not a "good Samaritan."

Lacan ends his paper on the mirror phase by saying that it is only when we depart from these traditional or idealizing forms of friendship or love, that the true voyage begins.

> The suffering of neurosis and psychosis are, for us, the school of the passions of the soul. . . . Psychoanalysis alone recognizes this knot of imaginary servitude that love has always to undo again or to cut free. For such a task, the altruistic sentiment is without promise for we who bring to light the agressivity that underlies the action of the philanthropist, of the idealist, of the pedagogue, and even of the reformer. . . . Psychoanalysis can accompany the patient to the ecstatic limit of "*You are that*" in which is revealed to him the cipher of his mortal destiny, but it is not in the power of our practice alone to bring him to this moment in which the true voyage begins.[20]

One may take these sentences from 1936 as announcing the start of *Lacan's* voyage, the beginning of the destiny of *his* style and *his* difficulty: it supplied the angle from which he was to undertake his long and laborious rereading of Freud.

The central activity, especially in the early years of the Seminar, was an exegetical one. Lacan set out on a new intricate reading of the works of Freud. The purpose was to return to the *sens*, the meaning or direction, of psychoanalysis, before it had taken the "idealizing" orthopedic form it had assumed in America. Lacan's aim was thus not the "progressivist" one of establishing or consolidating the "advances" in the discipline; it was rather a matter of going back to the writings that had founded it. And yet this "return to Freud" was not a conservative preservation of doctrine, and did not issue in a defense of Freudian orthodoxy. The psychoanalytic movement would have completely dissipated itself, Lacan declared, were it not for *l'événement-Freud*—the event of Freud. And this event is to be found nowhere else than in

Freud's writings. "The writings *are* the event; they participate in the temporality inherent in discourse."[21] Freud's writings are like the "shelter" of his thought or philosophy, like embers burning faintly in a convent. To return to Freud was to return to these embers in the convent of psychoanalysis. It was to say again what psychoanalysis is, should be, had never stopped being despite its misconceptions of itself: a new ethic.

Two general claims underlie this conception of psychoanalysis. In the first place Lacan stressed the singularity of Freud's concept of the unconscious as a "fundamental concept." The unconscious is not an added characteristic to our thoughts or our minds; it is a completely novel view of what our thoughts and minds are, and of their relations with our bodies. We cannot even *identify* it within our received vocabularies or practices, for it constitutes an "event" in them.

Philosophical interpretations of Freud at the time had attempted to cast his thought into a more familiar philosophical vocabulary; Ricoeur and Sartre each read Freud in terms of the philosophical languages and assumptions that supplied their points of departure. Lacan moved in the opposite direction of defamiliarizing the views we might start with. He stressed the ways Freud's conception of the unconscious did *not* fit within any received philosophical or medical terminology; he tried to show how Freud's language did not overlap with any we already know. And he suggested that it was a symptomatic weakness of these paradigms or vocabularies that the precise sense of the unconscious could not be stated within them. To read Freud was to see how novel and singular his discoveries were, to rediscover what no one had conceived before. It was to begin to see in just what way the intricate irrationalities of our words and our bodies are more important to who we are than our "vaguely policed personalities."

In the second place, Lacan held that this novelty or singularity of the Freudian concept of the unconscious was an ethical one. "The status of the unconscious is ethical."[22] The "event" in Freud's thought was an event in ethics.

Under the Freudian concept of the unconscious, "the subject" was not what Aristotle had called a "psyche," a functional principle of life in the body; for it introduced a non-functional libidinal principle of the body in the way one lives one's life. It was not what Descartes had called a "thinking" or mental substance, since "it thinks where I am not," and, in particular, in the destinies of "my" body, where "I" am not. It is not something that can be inferred from a general theory of Humanity, for it is particular to each subject.

And this event in philosophical psychology was also an event in ethical purpose. Psychoanalysis is not an ethic of *intentions* or *the will* (the unconscious is not a weakness or failure of the will). It is not an ethic of *actions* and their predictable consequences (unconscious symptoms are actions whose descriptions and consequences no one wants to know anything about). It is not an ethic of basic *needs* and the adjustment of social arrangements to meet them (there is no social arrangement that could eliminate the fact of the unconscious). Psychoanalysis replaces a psychology of intentions, actions and needs with a "theory of the unconscious"—of our non-anatomical bodily destinies, our symptomatic acts, and in a singular and central way, the difficulties of our words. The kind of difficulty it introduces into ethical thought is thus not one that can be resolved by more subtle ways of distinguishing reasons from causes, "is" from "ought," passion from reason. For its aim is not to make us more virtuous citizens or more productive workers. It is not an attempt to insure that our actions contribute to the good of all, or of determining which principles we cannot rationally disagree with. It is not an aim that can be realized through the institution of positive laws or moral sanctions.

The difficulty of "teaching" about the unconscious is thus twofold. There is the difficulty of the singularity of the concept of the unconscious in our thought; and then there is the singular difficulty which, under this concept, we would have in our living—the difficulty of that of which the unconscious is the *aveu*.

The Freud-event is to have read what in neurosis is the *aveu* of the subject: namely, that this *aveu* is nothing else than the hole through which all Other is separated from *jouissance*: understanding by that all that cannot accede to it without his *aveu*.[23]

Lacan's "authorization" of himself thus came through his relation—one might say his "transference"—to Freud, the *author*. The incredible importance Lacan attached to close attention to the "letter" of Freud is tied up with this fact. It seems more decisive than the relation Lacan had to Freud through his analysis with Lowenstein. As a founder of a "School" of psychoanalysis (albeit an unofficial one), Lacan is distinguished in not following the pattern of filiation through training analyses which characterize the rest of psychoanalysis, at least for the first generation. In breaking with this sort of filiation, Lacan was free to try to transform the institution by transforming the place of Freud's writings in it. Perhaps this fact is connected with another: Lacan breaks with the predominantly Jewish-Protestant composition of the analytic community, with its roots in German culture; he introduced the writings of Freud to a more Roman Catholic France.

In the heady year of 1969, following the events of the previous spring, Foucault helped to establish a foothold for Lacan's teaching in the new campus of the University of Paris in the Château of Vincennes. There exists a transcript of Lacan's own appearance there. In a heated exchange, he declared to his radical student audience that

> the aspiration to revolution has but one conceivable issue, always, the discourse of the Master. That is what experience has proved. What you, as revolutionaries, aspire to is a Master. You will have one.[24]

Such was the moment of the marriage of Lacanian psychoanalysis and radical politics, and the start of what would become "French feminism."

In the same year of 1969, in a paper called "What is an author?" Foucault presented a perspective on the epistemological peculiarity of Lacan's reading of Freud, or his relation to Freud, the author. Foucault suggested that we might regard Marx and Freud as authors of a particular sort, that had emerged in Europe in the nineteenth Century. The sort of "discursivity" they introduced would be characterized just by the manner in which it could be altered through a novel commentary of its paradigm or founding writings. In the case of original scientists like Galileo, Cuvier or Saussure, it was only the subsequent "normal science" that corrects and determines what is significant in the founding or paradigm texts. "[T]he founding act of a science can always be reintroduced within the machinery of those transformations that derive from it."[25] That is why a close reading of original texts is not central to the investigations to which they give rise. "Reexaminationof Galileo's texts may well change our knowledge of the history of mechanics, but it will never be able to change mechanics itself."[26] By contrast, Freud and Marx would have written things which matter not just to the history of the discipline, but to the discipline itself. "The work of initiators of discursivity is not situated in the space the science defines; rather it is the science, or the discursivity, which refers back to their work as primary coordinates."[27] That is why "reexamining Freud's texts modifies psychoanalysis itself, just as a reexamination of Marx's would modify Marxism."[28]

And yet in Lacan's "modification" of psychoanalysis through his reexamination of Freud's texts, there is an even more complex way of thinking of Freud "as an author." For Lacan asked himself how, before Freud had become the founder of an institution and a "movement," he had himself become an "author"—how he came to put "himself" into his work and his conception of his work, how he introduced into it his "self-analysis" conducted in an epistolary manner through his transference with the odd Berlin nose doctor, Robert Fliess. For, as Lacan stressed, it is after all his *own* dream, and his own dream of himself as an analyst, with whose interpretation Freud inaugurates his *Interpretation of Dreams*.

In effect, Lacan said that the central "event" throughwhich Freud was to become the author of those writings which we now call "psychoanalytic," was his encounter with *hysteria*. "It was the hysteric who taught Freud about the unconscious."[29] Freud's becoming-an-author would start in France, in the clinic of Charcot. Such was the site of the event that would cause Freud to break with, or at least to question, his own Viennese anti-vitalist medical training.

In Freud's dream about getting Irma to accept the injection of his "solution" to her difficulties, and in the tense drama he restaged in the Dora Case, we find Freud engaged in a great struggle over the *aveu* of the hysteric, in which Freud's own worries about securing acceptance of his work as "science" seemed to him to be at stake. For these hysterical women obliged Freud to remove the very concept of a "symptom" from a medicine of anatomical localization, making it instead a property of the idiosyncratic ways the hysteric at once masked and gratified her desire with her body and her words. They thus obliged him to ask what "the subject" must be for this kind of symptom-formation to be possible. And with this change in the conception of the symptom and its subject, went a new conception of the aims of its treatment: an "analysis" was something other than diagnosis and prescription. It became a matter of responding to the other's "desire," of adopting a sort of suspension or *epoche* in the face of that desire, which would allow for a neutral "floating" way of listening—a neutrality and a listening that would create the space of "transference" that would structure the work of rearticulating this desire in "concrete discourse."

Freud's encounter with hysteria was thus an epistemological event, since it caused him to abandon or qualify what his medical training had taught. It was also a "self-analytic" event, since it caused him to reexamine his own desires, and their role in his new practice, to the point of recognizing the problem of his own "counter-transference." It was also something of a "literary" event, since it caused him to invent new ways of writing up a case-study (whose "prurient" interest he feared), and of composing a scientific treatise on dreams that included an analysis, according to that science, of how it was discovered. But Lacan stressed that the encounter with hysteria was in just these ways and at the same time an *ethical* event. As he pointedly put it, were it not for his encounter with hysteria, Freud would have remained an *idealist*: "I would say that Freud would certainly have made a perfect impassioned idealist had he not devoted himself to the other in the form of the hysteric."[30]

For his encounter with hysteria obliged Freud to see that in one's "symptoms" one desires something other than one's good, and that this "other satisfaction" was something inherently rebellious to the medical norms of health. In her sexuality, the hysteric was a defiance of the "mastery" of medicine, its claim to know what was good for her. For the other satisfaction the hysteric flaunted with her "symptoms," was one for which there could be no generalized, ideal, "normal" manifestation. In some sense, the question of the hysteric was the question of enclosing sexual desire within the norms of a proper "healthy" satisfaction. The "symptoms" of the hysteric were not to be defined by reference to an ideal of a healthy sexuality; it was, on the contrary, the ideals of health that had to be rethought in order to come to terms with the sort of "desire" Freud came to think those symptoms gratified. Freud's theoretical question—What must the subject be in order for such symptomatic satisfaction to be possible?—was also an ethical one: What to do about this desire for which there was no "cure"?

There is thus an ethical sense to this new relation to medicine. In ancient Schools of Ethics, medicine and philosophy went together, for it was thought that what was good or virtuous to do was always connected to what, medically speaking, was good for one. *Mens sana in corpore sano*. Something of this tradition is preserved in our contemporary preoccupations with the holistic "wellness" promised by the "alternative medicine" of a "new age"—of which Lacan said it leaves our *jouissance* cold.

In short, through his self-analysis (which he reports having dreamt about as a medical dissection of his own body), Freud would have departed from the tradition in modern medicine Foucault had analyzed in 1962 in *The Birth of the Clinic*. But while Freud broke with this medicine that identified health with absence of pathology in the individual organism, he refused to revert to the earlier holistic medicine revived in hypnosis, spiritualism, the laying-on of hands, and eventually, the archetypes of the collective unconscious.

Lacan presents the "homeostatic" or "hydraulic" models of Freud's speculations as in effect resorting to the earlier character of medicine, where what is good is good for you. "What else is this famous least tension through which Freud articulates pleasure than the ethics of Aristotle?"[31] Conversely he takes Freud's speculations that there exists something "beyond the pleasure principle," connected with an inherent aggressivity, as departing from such an ethic. For if aggressivity belongs to our identity, our relation to ourselves *supposes* our relations with others, and cannot be conceived as an isolated perceptual "apparatus." Lacan emphasizes what in Freud's account of our drives inserts us into this fatal imaginary passion, for which there is no cure. For Lacan, if Freud was a "biologist of the mind" it was thus in the sense that he discovered something in the body that endlessly troubled the mind, something that goes "beyond" what the mind conceives or calculates as its good. The ethic of Freud's medicine was the ethic of this endless difficulty. And it is to this difficulty that Freud would have alluded when he declared that psychoanalysis was an "impossible task."

The difficulty of Lacan's teaching or his style was to provide for the "school" of this ethic, or of this "impossible task." It would not be a school whose master teaches how to overcome the ignorance of each as to what is good for all. It would rather be the school of a master who not only refuses the knowledge of such a Good or Ideal, but who makes the eros of our not-knowing the principle of a new kind of medicine, a new kind of philosophy.

Lacan was the orator who taught of the difficulty and the violence of our relation to our ideals, and of the passion and the cost of saying the truth about ourselves. He was the orator who introduced this difficulty and this passion into the very conception of contemporary philosophical activity. He wrote no book; he left no fixed doctrine or principle of conduct. He left to those formed by his teaching to establish, if they could, the "book" of the ethics of this strange new "master in thought."

What then is philosophical difficulty? The later Wittgenstein spoke of the difficulties that arise when language takes a holiday from its ordinary, practically-rooted uses, entangling itself in ways it would take a whole "therapy" in thought to undo. The later Heidegger thought he was confronted with another sort of difficulty, that of releasing philosophical thought from a "metaphysical" preoccupation that would have dominated its destiny in the West, rediscovering a primordial "poetry."

Perhaps difficulty in philosophy is not always the same. A philosopher must discover or define "his" or "her" difficulty, and this difficulty becomes what is most distinctive about his or her philosophy. That is why philosophical difficulty is more than conceptual or rhetorical difficulty; it is also "subjective."

Perhaps to start to think is to find oneself in a peculiar difficulty one knows not yet how to define. And the problem of "style" in a philosophy is the problem of finding the words and the acts appropriate to the difficulty one thus discovers or brings to light. In any case, the styles of Foucault and Lacan are difficult not simply conceptually or rhetorically, but in this "subjective" philosophical sense as well: a difficulty with "themselves" in the exercise of their thought. It is that which makes of each of them, not just a brilliant historian or an original therapist, but a philosopher. But what is distinctive in their philosophies from this perspective, is that each connects the difficulty he discovers to the ancient question, for which the enigmatic figure of Socrates stands: What is the eros of doing philosophy?

Indeed it is just in tying the philosophical passion for the truth to their peculiar "difficulties with themselves" that they offer a distinctive image of philosophy and a new sort of *philia*. The *philia* of philosophers would not lie in common love for the Idea, but in the passionate confrontation of their difficulties—with themselves and with one another. To examine, discuss, question or "read" the thought of another philosopher "philosophically," would thus not be to reconstruct his doctrine or his Idea, but to isolate and to rethink his difficulty. Philosophical friendship would be the passion of understanding the difficulties of others in terms of one's own, and one's own in relation with others. Such is the sense in which Foucault and Lacan would have been friends. Each refrained from pronouncing on the work of the other, preferring instead to reinterpret or reintroduce the other's difficulty in terms of his own.

One might thus say that their difficulty for *us* lies not so much in their doctrines as in their passions: in the kind of "experience of thought" they tried to define. That is why we might read them again today, not as authors of implacable monolithic systems of thought, but as open-ended or unfinished exercises and experiences in thought. To read them in this way is to rediscover something of the passion of their thought, and to raise again the ancient question of the passion of philosophy.

In rereading the two in terms of their difficulties, I have thus sought, in this book, to isolate and define a difficulty or a question which their work leaves us: the question of what ethics is, has been, might be for us today.

Part 1
Lacan

In psychoanalysis nothing is true except the exaggerations.
—Theodore Adorno

It happened that I did not publish *The Ethics of Psychoanalysis* . . .
With time I learned that I could say a little more about it. And then I
realized that what had constituted my path *(mon cheminement)* was of
the order of *je n'en veux rien savoir* (I-do-not-want-to-know-anything-
about-it). That is no doubt what makes it that, with time, I am here
still (encore), and that you too, you are here *still (encore)*.[1]

This is what Lacan told his Seminar in 1972; these are the first words
of his *Encore*. They suggest that the Seminar on Ethics, the only one
he wanted to write up as a book, enjoyed as special place in his oeuvre;
he would have continued along his singular path, his *cheminement*,
just because he would never be able to be done with it.

The Seminar on Ethics was delivered in 1959–60. It was the time of
the Algerian War and the political idealism it carried with it; and Lacan
arranged to have the portions of the Seminar devoted to Antigone sent
to his step-daughter, Laurence Bataille, then in jail for her part in the
struggle for Algerian independence. It was also a dramatic moment
for Lacan, and for psychoanalysis in France, following the famous
Discourse Lacan had delivered in Rome six years earlier, which had
become a sort of manifesto of a split in the analytic institution. Lacan
was the hero of that fateful institutional battle. And in the Seminar,
Lacan presents Freud as a kind of hero: the hero of a "revolution" in
ethical thought, who taught of a "discontent" in civilization for which
there exists no salvation and no reconciliation; the hero of a new kind
of ethical practice that might respond to the "tragedy" in our modern
progressivist, scientific, "enlightened" culture.

There had been talk of tragedy following the unspeakable brutalities
of the War. Sartre had said that in their uncritical enthusiasm for

consumption and free enterprise, Americans lacked the "tragic sense." Lacan thought as much of the "ego-psychology" of the New York School, through which psychoanalysis had "adapted to the reality" of America.

In connecting this "tragic sense" with the Freudian discovery of an inherent "discontent" in our desire, Lacan sought to introduce it into the domain of ethics in a new way. Philosophically or intellectually, the "tragedy" of the European World War had been understood through Marxism and Phenomenology. These two kinds of thinking, as it were, had taken the place of ethics.

But it was ethics that preoccupied Lacan. It was the whole conception of what our ethics are, which, he held, we needed to rethink. What was new or original in Freud was to have reconceptualized and reoriented our sense of ourselves as ethical beings, promising something new, something other we might yet become. Thus, in these years in Gaullist France, Lacan declared to his Seminar that this promise of the Freudian "revolution" was before us *still*: the promise of something new in the ethics of our desire, our love, our *eros*, the strange beauty of an original modern "erotic."

A Revolution in Thought

"The revolution in thought (*pensée*) that the effect of analytic experience brings with it concerning the ethical domain,"[2] was thus, for Lacan, a revolution in our very conception of this domain. One domain of ethics had been the ends of virtue, another had been the rules of duty. Each had invented one way of raising the question of moral knowledge, or of what it is for us to have, or to acquire, a true *logos* about our lives. Why is one goal or good rather than another rational or wise for me to pursue? How can I know which rules or principles are rational for me to follow?

If, in ancient ethics, the rules of duty revolved around the ends of virtue, for Kant it was the other way around: the good revolves around the supreme principle of obligation. Freud would then have introduced a third "revolution," redrawing the map of the terrain of ethics. Kant had made duty abstract, separating it from all "pathology," from anything that happens to us as sensual beings. The problem for Freud would be to rediscover the connection between ethics and "pathos" or experience, without reverting, as in ancient wisdom, to a supposed knowledge of the good. In this revolution, Freud would then reconnect ethics and eros in a new way: both the knowledge of the good life and the abstract rationality of the moral law would revolve around the "desire" to which each of us gives testimony in his unconscious.

> [Freud] set out, or set out again, from the ancient step of philosophy: namely that ethics can not derive from pure obligation. Man in his acts tends towards a good. Analysis puts desire back into favor as the principle of ethics. Even censorship, at first the only thing of desire to figure as morality, draws all its energy from it. There is no other root of ethics.[3]

The "step" ancient philosophy had taken in ethics was to raise the question of how to best live one's life. But what a "life" is, and what it means to lead or conduct or live it, have not always been conceived in the same manner. To live a life has meant to discover an essential nature or purity, to respond to one's fate or destiny, to acquire self-sufficiency or autonomy, to maximize one's pleasures and so forth. The question of how best to live has varied with the conceptions under which people have placed their lives and their living. In postulating the existence of the unconscious, Freud was, in effect, offering a new picture of what it is to live one's own life, to inhabit one's world, and to maintain relations with oneself and others: this *unheimlich* world in which the ego is not the master of the house, or in which "the subject is *chez lui* in the unconscious."

If Freud thus set out again on the ancient step of ethics, it was by reintroducing the problem of *eros* in our lives: the question of ethical knowledge, the question of giving a true *logos* or account for one's life, would become an erotic problem. For the unconscious *is* a strange and laborious sort of knowledge about our lives which we have repressed or forgotten; and the transference that structures the erotic "bond" of an analysis follows from the place this desire has in our living, of which the unconscious is the knowledge. As Lacan put it in 1959:

> Why does analysis—which has brought such an important change in perspective about love in placing it at the center of ethical experience,

which has brought such an original note, certainly distinct from the mode under which love had until then been situated by moralists and philosophers in the interhuman relation—why does not analysis push things further in the direction of what, strictly speaking, we must call an erotics? There is something that merits reflection.[4]

This remark occurs in the midst of the picture of an analysis with which the Seminar on Ethics opens: analysis is a *démasquage*, an "unmasking" of the relation a subject has to the "truth" of his desire; it is made possible by a bond of love, the bond of transference; and it aims at a certain "non-dependency" or freedom. And yet this unmasking, this bond of love, and this sort of freedom do not suppose or prescribe any norm for living. For what is "unmasked" is not a generalizable good for all; the form of love that structures the unmasking is not an altruism, or a sympathy that supposes knowledge of such a good; what incites one to engage in it is not an abstract duty independent of all experience of oneself; and the freedom it offers one is not a self-sufficiency or a self-mastery.

Unmasking the truth in analysis is thus not rooted in a general normative theory as to who we should be or what we must do. Psycho-analysis is not a *sagesse*, a general wisdom as to what it is good to be; it is not a *morale*, a theory of a general principle or rule of what it is right to do. On the contrary, it raises new questions about the place of desire in the demand of Wisdom, and in the nature of obedience to the Law of Duty, and so introduces a new task. In imagining the Cities of the Good or the Republics of Duty, philosophy has sought to rational-ize what is good for us, or the moral rules we must observe. Freud raised the question of the place of "desire" in our ethical cities and moral republics, and of the place of "discontent" in our "civilization." What can we make of ourselves in virtue of this "discontent" which the effect of analytic experience reveals?

The picture Freud offered of what it means for us to live was thus a "tragic" one. It is a picture of a traumatic libidinal necessity that exposes us to the fortune of our destinies and so divides us from ourselves and one another. It is a picture of a basic "morbidity" that cannot be averted by anything we can know or calculate as our good. The stories we tell of our lives, and which we can never stop writing in them, would betray this "truth" about us, this *aveu* of what it is that we love without knowing it.

The Life of the Body

A basic principle of psychoanalysis is that our life, even and especially "the life of the mind," is an *embodied* life. But this embodiment is of a peculiar sort. Our bodies have a part in our lives we had not recognized. We *think* with our bodies in ways we had not realized.

Analytic philosophers have conducted thought experiments to determine whether or not we think we need ourbodies to individuate or identify us: Could Jones start living in Smith's body? But in these conceptual experiments, the body has figured as the physical organism, or later as the physiological "hardware" our minds would "program."

The Freudian or libidinal body would individuate us in our living in another, non-physiological manner: it would submit each one of us to a particular destiny that confronts us as an enigmatic compulsion we don't know what to do about. For our Freudian "embodiment" is a fundamentally traumatic one, and the unconscious is the way this trauma works itself out in the particularities of the living of each one of us. That is why a "collective unconscious" is a contradiction in terms.

Hysteria shows that if we think with our bodies, it is in idiosyncratic ways which no anatomy can classify. But what Freud called erogenous zones are no more anatomical than are the hysterogenous ones. The libidinal body is not the same thing as the anatomical or physiological body, and has another sort of relation to our living.

Nor is the libidinal body the instinctual body. For "drives," unlike instincts are not tied to specific conditions of satisfaction, but are submitted to an open-ended "plasticity," ever susceptible to "substitutions" in their objects and aims. Our drives are constantly missing their aims and deviating from their objects, and that is why our "desire" is not a "need" identifiable by what satisfies it.

Freud thus spoke of the "vicissitudes" or "destinies" of our bodily drives, picturing them as "broken paths"—paths in our living that are not internally ordered or predetermined, but which "break" against the events that cause them to return on their histories and start up again. Even "affects" like anxiety, depression or the "unconscious feeling of guilt," are not immediate mental states, but rather states of the libidinal body that go beyond the subject that experiences them, discovering a complex connection with his peculiar bodily destinies.

Our Freudian or libidinal "embodiment" is thus both "perverse" and "polymorphous." Our mouths, our anuses, our sexual organs, our gazes and our voices, are those bodily zones in our living that are the sources of a libidinal "energy" whose enigmatic destiny requires of us a singular retrospective interpretation. For Lacan, the basic sense of Freud's break with his thermodynamic or hydraulic models was the discovery of this non-methodical character of our bodily destinies: the "energy" that is thought to "push" the various drives through their vicissitudes is not one that can be calculated, but only interpreted after the fact in its effects.

It follows that while its effects can be interpreted, the "work" of the unconscious can never be measured or tempered as in a system of balances. And this is just what distinguishes it from the sort of destiny the body was thought to have in ancient ethical Schools, what distinguishes it from hedonism or from the Aristotelean mean.

The promise of analysis is thus not a "balanced life"but a sort of *savoir-faire* with this "incalculable" energy in our embodied living, whose effects cannot be known in advance, but only read in the complexities, the maladaptations, the suffering, which make our lives our own.

The Morbidity of Desire

Lacan thought that Freud's "pessimistic" speculations on the existence of a "death-instinct" play an essential part in his conception of our libidinal embodiment. Our desire is not only polymorphous and perverse; it is also "morbid." For through the singular destinies of the libidinal body, one would be seeking one's own dying; there is something in our living that prefers death. Thus at the start of his Seminar on Ethics, Lacan asserts that analytic experience, more than any before it, deepens our understanding of what the French psychiatrist Hesnard had called *l'univers morbide de la faute*.

It is for this reason, he declares, that we must count *Civilization and its Discontents* as fundamental work, essential for understanding the sort of beast with which one is confronted in an analysis. For in this work, Freud discovered that the superego (and its "culture of death") does not derive from social or psychological sources alone, but is a "structural" discontent of our own desire: its inherent "morbidity." The originality of Freud is to have shown that our ethical sensibility has its roots in this fact, and to have imagined a new way of conceiving our relation to it.

The category of the "morbid" was a category introduced by modern medicine. That was, at any rate, a central claim of Foucault's *The Birth of the Clinic*. In this book, he says that Freud didn't *happen* to be a philosopher as well as a doctor; it was rather that in its history, "medical thought is fully engaged in the philosophical status of man."[5] With what he calls "the Clinic," Foucault argued that modern medicine broke from a previous holistic tradition, defining health as the absence of disease in the organs of a particular body. The change brought with it a new attitude towards death. With Bichat, death was "individualized," or made an inherent property of the pathology of an individual body. At bottom, one does not die because one becomes sick; it is rather because one must die, that one falls ill.

The image of death "attacking life" was thus replaced with the image of a "pathological life," and death was imagined not as macabre, but as *morbid*. Thus the category of the "degenerate" became for the first time a positive medical category—the figure of life caught up in the process of its own self-destruction, much as in the morbid nineteenth-century figure of the "consumptive" genius. There was thus a profound alteration in the "philosophical status of man"; Bichat would be a start of the rather morbid idea that death is our "ownmost possibility."

As death became a question of individual "morbidity," disease broke away from the "metaphysics of evil" where it had been linked to the problem of "fortune" in living: "Death left its tragic heaven and became the lyrical core of man."[6] It became something that singularizes us from within, something that requires of our body "a style of its own truth."[7] In this respect, the new medicine of Revolutionary France would have rediscovered a Baroque experience of death and eroticism which, Foucault says, he will discuss in a subsequent work.

Lacan found this same Baroque sensibility in the category of the morbid in the thought of Freud. For, on the one hand, Freud linked the "silent" operations of an instinct for death to the fact that there can exist no rule to know in advance what strange vicissitudes our libidinal bodies will undergo. There is thus something "beyond," something "other" than what we think is good for us, and who we think we are, when we represent to ourselves what we think we want or need. "Beyond the Pleasure Principle" is not another principle of regulation, but something that is always interrupting the "binding" of our energy to our purposes, submitting our eros to a whole entangled history. On the other hand, Freud said that there is something fundamentally morbid in this "other satisfaction" that is peculiar to each and everyone of us. That is why the morbidity of our desire individualizes us, and why, in this sense, our death is always our own. Our "symptoms" are the interpretations of a fatality we cannot yet read, and the unconscious is the knowledge of this fatality at work in our lives.

Psychoanalysis thus introduces a new *kind* of problem for ethical reflection: not the ancient problem that we may live and act in ignorance of what is truly good for us, but the modern problem that there is something in our desire that goes beyond what would direct us to what we think we want for ourselves. In particular, it raises the question of *fortune* in our lives in a new way, for it links fortune not to the good we can know, but to the inherent morbidity in our desire which takes us on paths we can never regulate nor foresee. Psychoanalysis holds that the "truth" of our mortal destinies is not one for which there exists a general wisdom, a general means for adequating one's living to what is truly good for it. To give a true *logos* for one's life is thus no longer to know how to wisely master it, nor is it therefore to submit to a master who teaches us how.

A Causality of Fortune

What then is the fortune of this mortal eros in our living? Lacan took this to be the problem of a kind of causality irreducible to either a social or a psychological determinism. In what sense do our libidinal bodies *cause* our symptoms, these maladaptations to which our dreams, our compulsions, the stumblings in our acts and tongues, would bear witness?

For Freud, this was the problem of "psychical causality" or of the effects of the events that break open new paths in the network of our psychical apparatuses. Following Lacan, Jacques-Alain Miller reconceptualized it as the problem of "metonymical causality": the libidinal body would be neither a mechanical nor an expressive cause of our symptoms, but the "displacement" within a structure caused by a fundamental or constitutive absence or lack in it.

Lacan, however, introduced the question of causality into an ethical setting. He connected the problem of cause to the ancient problem of knowing how to respond to what happens to us. He connected it to ancient reflections on fortune, luck, or chance in living, to *tuche* and thus to the concept of *kairos*, the opportune moment, the *"bon-heur."* He tried "to put the accent on the encounter in the specified sense of *bonheur*, or of the Greek *tuche*, at the expense of the automatism that belongs to all function of adequation."[8] Thus "psychical causality," or "metonymical causality" would be a "tuchical causality," a causality of fortune. Psychoanalysis would rediscover the sense in which "development is entirely animated by accident, by the obstacle of *tuche*, insofar as *tuche* brings us back to the same point at which pre-Socratic philosophy sought to motivate the world itself."[9]

Lacan was not alone in returning to the ancient theme of *tuche* in moral philosophy. Quite independently, Bernard Williams formulated it as the problem of "moral luck." As did Lacan, Williams connects the importance of the problem to the insufficient attention paid by moral philosophers to ancient tragedy. For it is in tragedy that one would find the incompatibility between the philosophical ideal of self-sufficiency and the "imperiousness" of contingency, fortune, *tuche* in our living.[10] More particularly, Williams finds that this incompatibility recurs in an "erotic" context: in the attempt to reconcile the passion of friendship with an ideal of self-control. Williams seems to have a stronger thesis: that it has been a "limit" of moral philosophy to have sought to tell us in advance how to respond rationally to whatever happens to us, and so to have asked of our reason to make of us autonomous or independent beings.

But in reinserting this ancient problem of *tuche* in a Freudian context, Lacan had something more precise and more dark in mind. In effect, he links the "fragility of goodness" to the "morbidity of desire." The reason our goodness is fragile is that our desire is morbid, and that is why our fortune and our destiny speak of a mortal truth that goes beyond any Aristotelean "excellence in living." Lacan's account of tragedy, and in particular, of *Antigone*, is, as we shall see, distinguished by this view.

Lacan took a decidedly dim view of the developmental story of "psychosexual" stages in a normal process of growth or maturation, whose deficiencies it would be the job of analysis to rectify. He declared that the great charts that tell personality-doctors what an infant must do and be at various ages in order to turn itself into a well-adjusted adult had no basis in biology. The erotic "events" of childhood with which Freud was concerned were not at all of this sort; and his aim in treating their effects in analysis was not at all that of acquiring the habits of the genitally mature adult.

On the contrary, talk of stages means only that our oral, anal, sexual, our gazing and vocalizing bodies, are constantly interrupting the regularities of our living, taking the occasion of what happens to us to undergo a process of frustration, repression and regression, through which they confront us again in new ways. It is through this rhythm that the "psychosexual" events of our past belong, if not to our biology, then to our "bios," our lives. They become those "nodal points" around which Freud said our symptoms grow like mushrooms in mycelium, where our living "straddles the unknown." Even affects like melancholy and mania are the response of our bodies to these events that break up our living and whose effects we cannot yet know.

Lacan took Freud's reconstruction of the "traumatic event" in the Wolfman case as exemplary of the role psychical events play in our lives. That event acquired its significance, or became the event that it was, only after the fact—*nachträglich*—through the symptomatic recastings Freud sought to unravel. Lacan thus referred to the "subjectivizations of the event which seemed necessary to explain at each turning point where the subject restructures himself."[11] That is why the "operations of analysis" would be "those of history in so far as history constitutes the emergence of truth in the real."[12]

The sort of events with which an analysis deals would be such "turning points" in our relations to ourselves and to others as mortal erotic beings. The aim would be to reconstitute the "truth" they thus

introduce in our *histoires*—a truth which always comes after and
with which we are never done. The events that make up our libidinal
destinies would be events of a particular kind. They are the events that
are "forgotten" in what we say and do, and in who we are and become.
They are the recurrence or insistence of something in those *histoires*
that we can never yet recount. Our unconscious is the memory of what
we have forgotten.

It is this Freudian conception of events that Lacan wanted to reintroduce into the ancient discussion of *tuche* or fortune. The "fortune" of
what happens to us would not, as Aristotle thought, be "defined by
being able to come to us only through being capable of choice, *proairesis.*"[13] It would rather be a matter of a "missed encounter," *une
rencontre manquée*. Events occur too early, or their effects come too
late, for us to be able to "assimilate" them in the portion of living that
is governed by *proairesis*. Thus they remain *en souffrance*, recurring
in symptomatic form. The problem of fortune is that things happen to
us which we can't regulate, and so we "forget" them and repeat them
in the disorder of our lives.

But, if our fortune is not a simple matter of Aristotelean *proairesis*,
it is not either a matter of determinism. Libidinal necessity, this great
ananke, does not determine or predetermine what we become. Rather,
it puts the unconscious to work; it supplies the unconscious with a
chance to work. Libidinal necessity, Lacan says, means that our bodies
never stop "writing themselves" in our destinies. Thus, though our
fortune as erotic beings can never be foretold, the way it works itself
out in the "censored chapters" of our histories can be interpreted. The
"law" of "psychical causality" is then neither social nor psychological,
but "structural."

The Laws of Our Desire

If there is thus a "law" of our destiny, a law of the "fatality" or
"morbidity" of our desire, it has this peculiarity: we cannot know it
in advance. The art of reading it is not an art that subsumes what
happens to us under a general regularity. For the law of desire is not
a general principle of which one would be ignorant; on the contrary,
it lies precisely in the effects of occurrences we cannot place under a

general rule. That is why it is unlike what Hume called a "habit." Freudian *tuche* is incalculable or improbable chance. To read it is not to know how to predict and control it.

Thus Lacan says "the Law" is not general, but "structural." It doesn't *happen* to desire; it "structures" the singular way desire "happens" in our lives. But if the law of desire is not a regularity, it is also not an interdiction, a sanction, a command that forbids. Freud held that all "secondary" repression rests on a "primary" one. Lacan reads this as meaning that the particular laws that sanction or forbid derive from a prior law that structures desire itself. This would be the premise of the fundamental and paradoxical Freudian discovery: that desire itself is the source of the moral law, the source of our moral obligation.

Early on, in a letter to Fliess, Freud wrote that he had the premonition that he was about to discover the origin of morality. He would tell the story of this origin through a kind of prehistoric fiction or myth. In *Totem and Taboo*, he thus recounts the famous murder of the "primal Father": it is when this dead father is turned into a "symbolic" one that our sense of moral duty would "begin."

We have interpreted the first rules of morality and moral restriction of primitive society as reactions to a deed which gave the authors of it the conception of crime. They regretted this deed and decided that it should not be repeated and that its execution must bring no gain. This creative sense of guilt has not become extinct with us. We find its asocial effects in neurotics producing new rules of morality and continued restrictions, in expiation for misdeeds committed, or as precautions again misdeeds to be committed. But when we examine these neurotics for the deed which have called forth such reactions we are disappointed. We do not find deeds but only impulses and feelings which sought evil but which were restrained from carrying it out. Only psychical realities not actual ones are at the basis of the neurotic's sense of guilt.[14]

There is, of course, a problem with this story: How could the brothers repent of their crime *before* the existence of morality? The crime occurs too early, or the moral description of it too late, for it to be able to properly occur in Freud's epic. Thus Lacan proposes to read it not as a description of an actual historical occurrence, but as a kind of modern myth. He gives it a "structural" interpretation, saying that

myth is "the attempt to give epic form to what operates from structure."[15] It is the "law of desire" to which Freud's tale would give epic
form. Our desire is so "structured" by repression that it appears to us
like a fundamental crime that occasions in us feelings of remorse or
guilt. What Freud's story would then tell us is that "repressed desire"
is basically a pleonasm, that the Law *is* our desire, is the imperious
necessity of our desire.

This law applies to each one of us. That is why if the neurotic is like
a private or asocial moral agent, a moral agent is a public, socialized
neurotic. If obsession, hysteria and paranoia are like distorted pathological versions of ourselves as moral beings, our images of ourselves
as moral beings are like idealized versions of these pathological conditions. And the principle that thus connects duty and pathology, the
principle that says that there is no duty without pain is this: our desire
is so structured by the Law as to make of us "obligated" or "guilty"
sorts of beings *before* we formulate just what our obligations or duties
are, and the principles that would govern them. Such would be the
great Freudian reversal in morality: we don't repress our desire because
we have a conscience; we have a conscience because our desire is
always and already repressed.

This reversal sheds a peculiar light on the long tradition in morals
that holds that our desire is what we must struggle against, must
restrain or control, in order to be good or to do right. The postulation
of the super-ego means that we gratify ourselves in such moral struggle;
it explains how our desire is gratified through the very idealization and
de-eroticization through which we come to demand of ourselves its
sacrifice. It explains why an "authoritarian" figure is not fundamentally
someone who lays down the law and says "no" to our desire, but
someone who assumes the idealized or de-eroticized role of such "authority," embodying the more basic law of our desire which always
obligates us in advance.

It is then in this "structural" sense that moral necessity, the necessity
of "I ought," is fundamentally a libidinal necessity and draws all its
energy from it. "Ought" is thus after all related to "is," but in a curious
way Lacan tries to capture with the ambiguity of *il faut*: "it must"/"he
fails." Putting desire back into favor in ethics thus raises a particular
problem: Can there exist an "I ought" or an "I must"—a responsibil-

ity—that is not just another command of the super-ego? Can there be an ethic of what in our being-obligated is prior to the formulation of any rule of conduct?

That is the question of the Freudian precept Lacan made his own: *Wo es war, soll ich werden*. For this *sollen* is something else than a *Schuldigsein*, and yet it not a simple *müssen*, something that causes or determines that I become. And the *ich* to which the precept is addressed is not an ego, not a generic entity the same in each of us; the precept is not in this sense an appeal to our "humanity." The *ich* is an "I" that does not yet, that *cannot* yet know who it is and what it will become. For the way "it" figures in our lives is through the improbable *tuche* of our fortune. The particular "ethical" problem with which psychoanalysis confronts us is, in short, the problem of not knowing the law of our own erotic fatalities.

It is a problem which previous ethical thought had sought to surmount in supposing that there exists something or someone who *does* know, someone or something that could adopt a "god's eye view" of ourselves and our destinies. Freud's discovery was the discovery of the *eros* that underlies this kind of supposition. The name which Freud gave to this supposition and the bond to which it gives rise is "transference." Transference is the supposition of a subject who would know. And in analyzing it, Freud found a way of letting us see something of our basic incapacity to know, to master or possess the law of our own desire.

Love, Truth and Transference

Psychoanalysis thus introduces the problem of a new kind of responsibility—the responsibility for our own desire. It involves a new kind of *eros*: that of telling the "truth" of this desire for which we can have no knowledge, but which is "written" in the puzzle of our destinies.

An analysis must expose the supposition that our desire is knowable. It must analyze the confidence or faith that somewhere or in someone there exists a knowledge of it. This confidence or faith is what Lacan calls our *bêtise*; the purpose of analysis is to deliver us from it. At the end of analysis what one would learn is that *no one* can know, not oneself, not even one's analyst. One senses the "presence" of the analyst, Lacan says, just when one credits him with knowing about this desire that is disturbing one. And it is the analyst's refusal of this confidence, or his not knowing, that would set the work of analysis going.

In Lacan's eyes, analysis would be the form of love which never supposes that it knows what is good for someone else; it would offer relief from the *bêtise* of all those who have always known better. In this way, it would be distinguished from *philia* and *caritas*. For *philia* is a love that brings men together in the knowledge of the good that is the same in each of us, and *caritas* supposes a knowledge of salvation or grace. Lacan remarks that Freud recoiled in horror before the commandment "Love thy neighbour as thy self." And Freud said that he was not sadistic enough to base his treatment in a sympathy for his patient's sufferings. Psychoanalysis is a form of love that is not based in those ideal parts of ourselves that would allow us to master our fate or to obtain salvation. On the contrary, it would open up even our first love, our love of ourselves, to a traumatic and fateful cause.

Lacan puts "soul" and "love" into a single *mot-valise*; he speaks of our *âmour*. Our souls would be inherently linked to our eros in a manner that is fundamentally traumatic. The bonds of association and identification which our *âmour* creates carry within them an aggressivity, a repulsion, a dissociation shown in what Lacan calls *hainamoration* (to be in love-hate). Tradition has taught us that love is what unites us in reciprocity, complimentarity or fusion. Freud, says Lacan, would teach rather that love is not what binds us together in a higher unity, but what "supplements" the hazards and the singularities of our libidinal destinies. For the truth of which our love stories speak is not fundamentally that of an ideal symmetry or fusion, but of this structurally enigmatic desire we would transfer onto the asymmetries of the bond of analytic work.

That is why the place of sex in Lacan's Freudian ethic is not that of a mutual, normal "genital love." Rather sex is perverse; it is morbid; it is traumatic. It occurs at the expense of those idealized self-relations that would unite us in the reciprocity of given equal positions, or in the mutuality in which we would compensate for what is lacking in one another. Sex is not the same in each one of us; it does not separate us into kinds or *genres* that complement one another. Rather sex singularizes us in our libidinal destinies, and so divides us from ourselves and one another. Thus there are no "undivided" sexual associations: *il n'y a pas de rapport sexuel*. That is why there can be no sex between completely self-sufficient beings, as there is none among angels or "Platonic" friends.

The eros of the practice of an analysis would thus introduce a new ethical question, the question of the responsibility to something that is prior to the just distribution of goods, and prior to the formulation of our obligations and their principles. It would be a responsibility to the "necessity" that is the law of our desire. This necessity is what Lacan calls "the real" as when he writes "the subject is the response to the real."[16] Freud's revolution in ethics can then be pictured as the process by which the eros of giving a *logos* to our lives is rerouted from the Ideal to the Real that is its source.

> ... a curious thing for a summary reflection that would think that all exploration in ethics must have as its object the domain of the ideal, if not the unreal, we go, on the contrary, in the opposite direction of a deepening of the relation to the real. The ethical question, in as much as Freud makes progress in it, is articulated by an orientation of the bearings (*repérage*) of man in relation to the real. To conceive of it, we must see what has happened in the interval between Aristotle and Freud.[17]

The Interval Between Aristotle and Freud

To conceive of the unconscious as an ethical category is to rethink ethics; it is to define it in distinction from previous conceptions of ethics. Lacan maintained that a reading of the great works of ethical philosophy should be required for the formation or training of analysts. But that reading would mark a contrast. Psychoanalysis, rather than being an idealism, moves in the opposite direction of deepening our sense of our relation to "the real." Freud would have introduced a new "realism" in ethics, as when he spoke of an analysis as an "education to the real."

In Lacan's idiom, *le réel* is not "reality." It is prior to the "reality-principle" and the attempt to adjust the "pleasure-principle" to it. It is more "external" to us than the "external world," since we constitute our ideal images of ourselves (that is ourselves) only by excluding it or separating ourselves from it. *Le réel* is rather *ananke,* libidinal necessity itself: it is this imperiousness of our own eros which psychoanalysis deciphers in our living. We can't avoid it, can't avoid *betraying* it in the symptoms which accompany our formative self-idealizations.

The "realism" of psychoanalysis is the realism of this necessity and its place in civilization. That is what distinguishes it from the philosophies in the interval between Aristotle and Freud. Psychoanalysis is an ethics "of the real," and confronts the "idealisms" of philosophical ethics with it. In our troubled libidinal existence it finds something that is prior to the "ideals" of Virtue, Duty and Utility, something which these ideals betray and which they cannot avoid. It takes Virtue, Duty and Utility as "idealizations" of the discontent inherent in civilization; it treats them as "fictions" in one sense Lacan gives to the term.

The sexual impasse secretes fictions which rationalize the impossible from which they derive. I don't say they are imagined; I read in them, like Freud, the invitation of the real which responds to them.[18]

The interval between Aristotle and Freud is a very long one, roughly coextensive with all of Western ethical thought. Apart from the question of Christianity, which assumes increasing importance as Lacan goes along, we may nevertheless distinguish three moments in that history which, for Lacan, introduce new questions or rework older ones—moments that are marked by the three great figures of Aristotle, Kant and Bentham. Each figure is a figure of a different *kind* of ethical thought, involving a different view of the ethical bond, of the nature of ethical knowledge, and of the features of our experience that matter for such knowledge or such a bond. There would thus be an ethics of the good or *eudaimonia,* of duty or the moral imperative, and of utility or the calculable consequences or actions of the rules that govern them. What Lacan then does is to offer a sort of "psychoanalytic portrait" of each figure, or a "psychoanalysis" of the fictions of each kind of philosophy: the Good, the Law and the Useful would appear as idealizations to rationalize our bearings in the real. What sort of bond, what type of obligation, and what new experience of pleasure or *jouissance* might come from the "invitation to the real" which Lacan, like Freud, would read in these fictions?

Aristotle's Friendship

Aristotle offers Lacan the supreme example of an "ethics of the Good." Aristotle taught that "the Good itself" subsists somewhere out there as the *telos* of all our various and sundry activities. Through proper patience and self-restraint, men may come to know this supreme and "syncategorical" Good. The Good is lacking in nothing; it is self-sufficient, and thus, in knowing it, men would no longer do harm to themselves and one another. For men are given to know, and to want to know, this Good by Nature herself. The most fully realized life, the one with the greatest potential for *eudaimonia*, consists in acting upon this desire for knowledge, which, as a man, one would possess by nature. True friendship, of which merely instrumental or pleasing relations are imperfect versions, is the bond that ties together those men who act upon the desire to know, thus discovering the harmony or accord with themselves and one another, which the universe has prepared for them. And such wisdom, such "friendship"—such "philosophy"—would be prior to the law of the City and its myths, even when it is deemed wise to observe such laws or myths, as in the case of Socrates' suicide.

Lacan is among those for whom such an "ethics of the Good" is no longer a real philosophical possibility for our modern scientific and industrial civilization; and he dreamt of no other civilization to restore it. Thus, when in 1959 Lacan informs his then largely clinical Seminar that they must read the *Nicomathean Ethics*, for they will rediscover in it the "field of experience" which they encounter every day, it is in part to mark a "discontinuity" or "distance": we can no longer think of ourselves as Aristotelean *psyches*, the excellence of whose activities would constitute "virtue."

The underlying "metaphysical biology" which supports the conception of *eudaimonia* as virtue in the natural task of the soul, and the soul as the living principle in the activities of the body, is no longer credible to modern Science. For the Nature known to modern Science is not intrinsically good, and does not reflect or indicate to us our basic *ergon*. And in order to know it, one does not have to know how to live well, to be virtuous, or discover the true harmony characteristic of *philia*. Alexander Koyré is Lacan's authority for the change. The closed meaningful world of ancient cosmologies would give way to an infinite universe of pointless particles; the natural world would no longer be thought to offer us an edifying spectacle: "Scientific discourse is something that owes nothing to the assumptions of the ancient soul. And it is from this alone that psychoanalysis arises."[19]

An ethical predicament would follow from this fundamental change in the conception of Nature: "our *bonheur* has no worthy place in either the macrocosm or the microcosm."[20] Psychoanalysis would offer a view of eros in this modern world where our *bonheur* or fortune has no cosmic support. In what Freud called our "sexuality" or our "libido," there is something fundamentally rebellious or inassimilable to our well-being or *eudaimonia*. It is not a matter of the virtues of a domestic or civic service to the aims of a *physis* that would reflect it. It is not something which, when moderated and restricted to appropriate occasions, serves to harmonize us with the world of our activities. On the contrary, it is fundamentally traumatic, and introduces something "beyond" our participation in such activities. For Freud, our *eros* is at odds with our *ethos*; its occurrence in our lives is always *unheimlich*.

Thus Lacan draws this contrast between the Freudian subject and the Aristotelean soul: for Aristotle the soul or *psyche* was "the sum of the body's functions," whereas for Freud "the subject of the unconscious is in touch with the soul via the body, here contradicting Aristotle—man does not think with his soul as the Philosopher thought."[21]

For Freud, the "thoughts" of the unconscious were like delegates that stand in for the body in its libidinal destinies. In this sense one "thinks" with one's body, and what provokes one to think in this way is something for which the soul has no use. Hysteria would testify to this: the unconscious "thoughts" of the hysteric are not those of her body's functions, but rather of a desire that defies any knowledge of such functions. And the same sort of "bodily" thinking would "happen to the soul with the obsessional symptom: a thought that burdens the soul—that it does not know what to do with."[22] Thus our libidinal bodies would be constantly introducing into our living thoughts that escape and burden our souls, interrupting the harmony with the world in which they find themselves.

Accordingly, Freud had a quite different notion from Aristotle of the sense in which our thinking may be said to "move" us in our various activities. As libidinal beings we would be "embodied" in a different way than as Aristotelean souls. What would "move" us would not be the needs or tasks defined by our ends or goods, but this imperious desire that breaks in on such needs, and opens the strange and entangled paths of our singular destinies. Our bodies would be moved by something beyond what in our souls might tend to our good, something other than this movement that can be generated or corrupted, but never interrupted and suspended in the processes though which we become who we are. Fundamentally, what would "animate" our bodies would be their relation to this "other satisfaction." Thus Lacan argues that we may think of our World as tending to a Good we can know, only to the degree that we have barred access to this sort of satisfaction, and the way it moves us.

> Thought is disharmony with the soul. And the Greek *noûs* is the myth of thought accommodating itself in conformity with the world, the world (*Umwelt*) for which the soul is responsible: whereas the world is merely the fantasy through which thought sustains itself—reality, no doubt, but to be understood as a grimace of the real.[23]

For Lacan, the distance that separates us from *eudaimonian* ethics lies in this "disharmony" of unconscious bodily thought with respect to the soul, this incompatibility between our eros and our ethos that would be characteristic of our modern scientific civilization and its "tragedies." Thus he sees Aristotle's doctrine of friendship as having the consistency of a great "fiction" that would "supplement" the basic impossibility, the basic *Unheimlichkeit*, of our libidinal existence—a fiction no longer credible to us.

Lacan's analytic portrait of Aristotle concerns, in the first place, the great "desire to know," which enjoys such a central place in Aristotle's conception of the relation of men to their good. A troubled eros would be at work in the tranquil reflective wisdom that infuses the notes Aristotle left for the leisured Lycenium lectures, to which men would gather, paying no fee, for the mere pleasure of "sharing in discussion and thought" concerning their happiness and their good. The lectures would not be an enactment of the desire for knowledge that would be natural to man, as the Philosopher thought. It is not the case that no difficulty, no *peine*, preceded this desire or worked itself out through it. On the contrary, Lacan maintains that it is precisely the sort of trouble that sets our bodies thinking that provokes us to want to know our good, and to know the Good from which it would derive.

Such indeed is one sense of his punning "translation" of *psyche* by *l'âme*. Inherent in our *âmes* would be this *âmour* that disrupts the more or less temperate pursuit of our good; and that is what makes the "fiction" that the world be just so ordered as to harmonize with this pursuit such a pleasing one. Thus it is not that the most fully realized life is the one that acts upon the desire for knowledge that Nature is kind enough to give us. It is rather that our *psyches* are formed through an *âmour* that troubles us and escapes our knowledge. That is why men would ever wish to attain a wisdom, and to enter into a friendship, in which this trouble would have no part.

The "philosophical" desire to know would thus have its source in the disturbance the libido introduces into our living. It would be the desire of the great *bêtise* which Lacan calls "transference"—the supposition of someone or something that knows. As such it would in fact go back to a remark Socrates makes in Plato's *Symposium*: I may not know the good, but I do know something about the eros of the search for it. Aristotle would, as it were,"naturalize" the pursuit for truth about whose eros Socrates thought he knew something. The supposition of Aristotle's teaching or *paideia* would be that it is of the very essence of the soul to seek this knowledge of which the impious men would be ignorant—just the desire that Socrates knew how to induce in the young men of Athens.

In his Seminar on Transference of 1960–61, Lacan would continue his discussion of ancient ethics through a minute commentary of the *Symposium*, the dialogue of the friendly contest in which men deliver to one another in turn great discourses on the nature of the Eros that possesses them. The "transferential" character of the discussion would be exposed by Socrates when he tells these men that Diotima had said to him one day that Eros is fundamentally a lack, and that to speak truly of eros, or to want to know it, is to speak from this lack. In this manner Socrates would displace the discussion of eros onto the prior question of the eros of such discussion. He would displace the question of eros onto a prior desire to *know* about it, and its relations with happiness or the good. And that is just what he himself would know best. It is what would make of him a new kind of master: the master of this desire-to-know, this pursuit of truth, that would submit men to a great *agon* with and among themselves, and so require of them a new *techne* and corresponding virtue. *Doxa* would no longer be enough to guide the conduct of free men, or the pursuit of their happiness.

For Lacan, this displacement was not so unlike the one Freud would discover centuries later in his erotic *agon* with the hysterical women of Vienna. In some sense the hysteric, and indeed anyone who enters analysis, would be in the Socratic position of not knowing his good, while knowing something about the eros of its pursuit. For, in masking her desire in symptoms whose meaning she could not say, the hysteric was demanding of her doctor that he tell her that meaning or produce the knowledge of the desire or eros that was possessing her. This demand is what established the bond and the struggle of transference dramatized in the Dora Case. Similarly it was just through an ignorance that Socrates (in whom Lacan detects a number of hysterical symptoms) induced in the eros of his young interlocutors a demand for a knowledge of the good they should pursue. "This is how Socrates can give birth in anyone to his knowledge, a knowledge, which, in fact, he didn't know. In this he resembles what Freud much later called the unconscious."[24]

It is from this sort of "transference" that would derive Aristotle's picture of a *physis* whose beneficent ends each man may discover in his soul, thereby finding that good to which his habits or his *ethos* should direct him. The Good Itself would, in effect, be a transferential entity, a vast subject-supposed-to-know; and it is thus that it would support the "patience of the soul in tolerating the world,"[25] for which the soul would be responsible in its being. The "sharing in thought and discussion" of philosophical friends would presume this Good, in much the same way as God would be the transferential assumption of prayer. "If Aristotle supported his God through this immobile sphere for the usage of which each follows his good, it is because it is meant to know that good."[26] And, for Lacan, what Aristotle called *philia* is thus "what represents the possibility of a bond of love between two of these beings" each of which "is in the world . . . to identify its good, its own good, with the Good that shines forth from the Supreme Other."[27]

What then is the nature of this "tension" in the soul's patient tolerance of the world, which it owes to the wisdom of the Supreme Other? What is the nature of this troublesome eros transferred onto the desire-to-know-the-good through which *philoi* would come to recognize and choose one another?

Lacan's portrait of Aristotle is of a man who wished to know nothing about perversion, nor, therefore, about sex. "What constitutes the body of sexual desire is simply classified by Aristotle in the dimension of monstrous anomalies: it is the term "bestiality" (or "brutishness") he uses concerning them."[28] Aristotle's ideal "virtuous" friendship would be a friendship "out-of-sex." "The *Horsexe*—there is the man upon which the soul speculated."[29] In the "speculations" of the souls of true friends there would be, as it were, something missing or lacking: the other partner. "What arises under the designation Aristotle offers of the sex relation," declares Lacan,

> is very exactly what analytic experience allows us to recognize as being, at least on one side of the sexual identification, the male side, as the object . . . that comes in the place of the missing partner (*le partenaire manquant*).[30]

Thus "sexuality" and "sexual identification" would be at issue in this ethics for which a common contemplation or "speculation" on a self-sufficient Good would constitute the greatest happiness available to man. "The morality of sexual behavior is the *sous-entendu* of all that was said of the good."[31]

That Aristotle's friendship was a friendship of "the man," and in this sense, a male friendship or "bonding," seems as noteworthy to us as it was unproblematic for Aristotle. The Philosopher modeled his view of *philia* on friendship among free men. Friendship with one's wife was to be made "proportional" to this bond, and friendship among women was hardly considered at all. And, of course, no one could be friends with a slave *qua* slave; indeed a slave could not even be friends with himself.

Moreover, the "manly" character of this ancient kind of bond or friendship was thought to be, as it were, underwritten by the Cosmos. The great problem of the active and the passive in matters erotic was supported by the metaphysics of Form and Matter: "this relation that was so fundamental, to which was referred each step of Plato, and then Aristotle, concerning what there is of the nature of things."[32] In particular, the "gross polarity" of active form and passive matter is to be found in the account of the origins of the Cosmos (and thus of the good), in the understanding of how the human species reproduces itself, and in the series of analogies that connect the cosmos to the city and the household, and thus to the *arche* in the soul. As such it was, for Lacan, "supported only by a fantasy through which they tried to supplement what can in no way be said, namely, the sex relation."[33]

A kind of male pederasty was at issue in this great metaphysical and ethical *agon* of "friendship." And there is a sense in which *philia*, in its very concept, was "homosexual" for Aristotle: he taught that it was incumbent upon friends to remain the same and to be alike, if not through equality, then through proportion. Indeed, for Aristotle, a true friend is "another soul." For the virtuous man relates to himself as to his friend, and he is friends with another just because he is his own best friend. By contrast, the impious or incontinent man, who cannot remain the same, can't befriend his own soul, or *a fortiori* that of another. That is why true friends need an *orthos logos*, and are the friends of it. For it is through such a *logos*, in which is evinced the highest sense of the soul's activities, that one most assuredly becomes steadfast or unchanging, and finds the accord with oneself that enables one to be friends with someone else who does the same.

This sameness and this alikeness, this *homos* in the bond of friendship which the *logos* assures, might then be contrasted with a "heterosexuality": a bond of love that would not have to bar access to the *âmour* of the partners, to this "other satisfaction" which the steadfast wisdom of self-sufficient friends would, at all costs, not want to know anything about. What Lacan calls the "missing partner" in the *philia* of virtuous souls is this Other that would in fact never let them be the same.

Thus, in Lacan's idiom, friendship-in-virtue was a matter of *l'âme âme l'âme*, a love or friendship not so much of one man for another, as a common love of "the Man" supposed in each. But, "as long as *l'âme âme l'âme*, there is no sex in the affair. Sex doesn't count. The elaboration from which it results is *hommosexuelle* as is perfectly readable in history."[34] And this kind of "man-sexuality" would be found among women as well: they too would come to *âme l'âme* in their partner, to the point of desperation, to the point of hysteria.

The "truth" of *philia* would thus reside in such perversity—such *âmoralité*. The lawless, bestial, disgraceful pleasures Aristotle wanted to eliminate as anomalies would be just the ones of which Freud would say the neurotic dreams—For how else, Lacan queries, could he "attain his partner?" *Âmoralité* would be the mark of something in the eros of "the Man" which departs from his *ethos*, from the patient performance of his *ergon* in city and household as in the rule of his own soul. It thus "subverts" the knowledge of his good, and the nature of things on which it would be based. For it binds him to a harm that is more than an ignorance of his good, or of the wise temperate performance of his role; it is linked to an "aggressivity" or a "mortality" inherent in his *âme* and his *âmours*.

For Aristotle, the "steadfastness" of the soul that would be the mark of its true virility, would, in particular, be displayed through exemplary contrast to the tearful "womanly" response to death, loss and mourning. In his suicide, Socrates would evince that philosophical courage that would prefer death to living in a world in which one would not be free to contemplate and realize the good. It is such courage that *philoi* would look for in one another. To become most fully a man, Aristotle taught, was to try to "immortalize" oneself and so imitate the Gods, and one would desire this immortality above all for one's friend as for oneself. By contrast, in the sort of *âmour* that would be the "truth" of this desire it is "mortality" that is at issue: *âmoralité* raises the question of a friendship that might recognize that harm or aggressivity inherent in the mortal character of *psyche* as *âme*, and thus would involve "the Woman."

Thus, when Lacan declares that "ancient speculation [followed] the path of what can manifestly only articulate itself as the good of the Man,"[35] his contrast is to the role "the Woman" would assume in Christian doctrine and mysticism. There, the "active" male sexuality would appear as an original "passivity" with respect to the Fault and the violence of its devilish temptations. God's Law would replace the philosopher's good, and a "charity," which requires the renunciation of the vanity of one's own good, and with it, the new practice of preaching, would turn to the most downtrodden, the most humble, the most "unequal" of men.

There is then a social or political consequence of this analysis of Aristotelean *philia* from the standpoint of Freudian *âmour*, a consequence Lacan rediscovers in ancient tragedy. For it follows that the household or city is not in its essence a harmonious living together in a natural or wise division of functions and tasks, but must in some manner come to terms with what in our libidinal existence must remain "disharmonious" in it, must remain "disproportional" or "unequal" to its noble totality: this other satisfaction in the life of our bodies. It is thus that even as we are "political animals"—or "domestic" ones— we remain beings troubled or "sick" in our eros or in our homes.

Conversely, there exists a kind of tyranny in supposing this Good that would harmoniously govern our domestic and civic live. There is a violence in this friendly desire for the true good, or the godlike immortality, of another. The fatal consequences of this tyranny or violence are the ones which (as we shall see) Lacan found dramatized in what was called tragedy, this art that is so close to analysis itself.

Thus for Lacan, Aristotle's ethics are not to be separated from his poetics. For the "well" in "living well" had an aesthetic or poetic sense: to live nobly, finely, beautifully. But whereas Aristotle taught that the life of contemplation of the self-sufficient Good was the finest or most noble life, tragedy would present us with a beauty in living, which could not know that Good itself, or which dispenses with the transferential *bêtise* of its supposition: a beauty born not of the immortality of knowledge but of the mortality of our *âmours*.

Thus tragedy supplied, as it were, the "primal scene" of philosophical ethics. Lacan would picture the famous rivalry between tragedy and philosophy in this way: before his leisured friends at the Lycenium, Aristotle taught of a Good which the free man would come to know, finding in it the source of his *ethos,* and in its contemplation, the highest *eudaimonia* of which the soul is capable. Against such a wisdom prior to myth or law, Lacan places the picture of a tragic universe, where the law in living is prior to the knowledge of the good, and fundamentally incompatible with it; where one can transgress the law without knowing it, or only knowing it after the fact, too late, as in the case of Oedipus Rex—a world in which knowledge is compatible with the harm and violence of fortune, and in which the ideal of the self-sufficiency of virtue carries a terror it cannot understand; the world for which the Good itself appears as a "grimace of the real."

Kant's Conscience

Kantian respect for the moral law is a different sort of thing from a common wisdom as to our good. Kant was radical in distinguishing the two. He said that there exists no general rule or principle for what is good for each and all of us. The task of moral philosophy should no longer be the vain attempt to supply us with such a principle, but should turn to something else: the nature of the law that governs our moral duties, and of its rationality.

Kant thought that all our particular moral actions or duties were ruled by a single great generic principle. But this principle was a "law" in another than this logical sense of its generality. It was also an imperative; it obligated people to freely apply it to themselves. It was Kant's view that the ground of this meta-obligation—the obligation to be moral—could not be rooted in prudential considerations, in our love for our good, or in our passions and compassions, indeed in anything in ourselves or our world that affects us.

It is this that Lacan admired in the great Kantian attempt to distinguish morality from prudence and instrumentality: "this radical separation of the pathological, of any regard for a good, a passion, even a compassion . . . through which Kant liberated the field of the moral law."[36] With this radical separation, the very conception of moral struggle was transformed. Our moral dignity or freedom would no longer be shown in overcoming a harm of which the immoral man is ignorant; it is rather that the moral agent must place himself under the aegis of a law-giving principle, without any regard for himself as a being in the natural world, and, in particular, in opposition to at least some of his natural inclinations.

Lacan's portrait of Kant concerns the role of the libido in this liberation of morality from "pathology." It would fall to Freud to analyze the peculiar eros that is involved in the "respect" we would have for the law, and for ourselves in as much as we "respect" it. Thus Lacan finds that an eroticism suffuses the *Critique of Practical Reason* to the point of comedy. Its spirit is captured in the title of his 1961 essay: "Kant with Sade."

What then is the nature of this submission to a law that would be freed of all that affects us? Kant's account of it is peculiar and even paradoxical in a number of ways, not the least of which is his view that our true freedom lies in this submission. Kant held that our observance of our moral duties cannot be based in sanction, in any reward or punishment, natural or divine: those would be merely prudential or instrumental concerns. Particular duties determine among possible actions which are permitted, which forbidden and which required. But simply to obey these duties is not worthy of our respect. For what we respect is a person's reasons or grounds for obeying them, or his relation to the law or imperative to follow them. To be worthy of respect, to be genuinely "moral," our submission to the moral imperative must be both "free" and "pure": the moral law is the sort of law that it is only if we freely apply it to ourselves, and the application is free only if we have no non-moral reasons for doing so. The moral imperative is thus "categorical," and Kant pictures it as a voice that would address each one of us individually, telling us to "act as if . . ."

How then do we respond to this curious imperious voice, and, in the first place, how do we represent its necessity to ourselves? It is nowhere to be found in our inner selves or in the world external to us. Our representation of it can never be merely subjective or objective. For the necessity of the "act as if . . ." cannot be transposed from the transcendental to the empirical plane without being turned from a categorical imperative into a hypothetical one.

The solution to this difficulty resides in the nature of the "as if" which the moral imperative never stops saying to us. The types, the examples, the symbols which we would make of ourselves in our moral activity would have the status of this "as if." They would be the "fictions" of our practical reason, and as such, would distinguish this reason from the theoretical kind, based on the "schematism" of the understanding. Thus the gap between the transcendental moral law and our observance of it would be bridged by "analogy." Our submission to the law would be *modeled* on the very laws of the "pathology" which we must exclude from it. Thus we must take the moral imperative *as if* it were an external natural law, *as if* our freedom in applying it to ourselves were a natural causation. But at the same time, we must judge *as if* the imperative came from within us. Our relation to it must be "spontaneous" since it is what it is only if we ourselves make it so; but it must also be "receptive" since it nevertheless confronts as a categorical imperative. Thus Kant says that the moral law confronts us at once *like* an external fear and *like* an internal inclination. What we exemplify in ourselves, and for one another, in our moral activity, can therefore not simply be good actions. In these actions, we must symbolically or analogically embody the empirically unrepresentable "law" that compels them.

An imperious voice that confronts us like an objectless fear and an unlocatable desire, the attempt to embody what this voice commands symbolically in our actions, displaying it in all the stories we tell of ourselves as moral beings—all this is rather familiar in the realm of the "pathologies" Freud identified or diagnosed. We find such a voice in obsession, where one is compelled by a law one knows only through a "free" or non-hypothetical application to oneself of elaborate rituals whose meaning and source escape one. It is shown in hysteria, where the necessity to freely show or exemplify oneself becomes a defiance of any "natural" knowledge about it and its origins. And in paranoia, an imperious voice speaks to one in such an enigmatic fashion that one becomes singled out for the mission of interpreting it for the rest of the world.

What is characteristic of such disorders is that the law or necessity that compels them is not to be found in the subject's representation of himself or his world, but is rather only shown in the symbolizations that comprise his "symptoms." In the ethics of psychoanalysis, one "judges" this necessity through the interpretation of the symptoms that manifest it and that "transcend" the subject's conscious interests or prudential considerations. But what one thus interprets in this ethical judgment is the subject's *desire*, his eros. One judges *as if* he gratified himself in his symptoms; the presumption is that in our symptoms, our eros confronts us *like* a law or necessity we can't represent to ourselves.

In postulating the existence of a "super-ego," Freud was in effect connecting the imperious "voice" of moral conscience to this necessity of our own desire that is shown in our symptoms, beyond our self-interest or prudence. The super-ego was Freud's way of analyzing how we gratify ourselves in our submission to the voice of moral duty, and how we can thus become "sick" from it. The super-ego is, as it were, Freud's demonstration of the inherent amorality—the *âmoralité*—of our conscience.

Freud's "second topography" that stages the interplay of ego, super-ego and id has often been read in the manner of the Kantian moral struggle: the super-ego would struggle with the demonic impulses of the id, as in Kant, duty struggles with inclination. Lacan argues that in fact Freud had a much more complex and perverse picture of the interrelation between the two, which in turn serves as a reading of the erotics of the Kantian struggle. This picture is captured in what Lacan calls the "paradoxical cruelty of conscience": the more one's conscience tends to become cruel, the less it is disobeyed; it becomes more exigent the more it is refined, more fastidious the more closely it tracks one down in one's innermost or unsuspected desires. This paradox betrays what Lacan calls the *gourmandise* of the super-ego—the more you feed it the more it wants. Lacan likens it to a parasite that feeds off the gratifications one affords it.

The cruelties of this rapacious hunger of the super-ego is then what is involved in Freud's discovery of an "unconscious feeling of guilt," and of a "moral masochism" in which pain figures not as punishment for disobedience to conscience, but as a condition for its very existence. And, indeed, there is a sort of perverse cruelty to the categorical imperative as Kant describes it. For, while this imperative can't be based in sanction, while no pain or sacrifice can ever be equal to it, it nevertheless, just because it is an imperative, presupposes our desire to transgress it. Our wills are not "holy" in the sense Kant gave to the term, the holy will being the one whose good actions require no imperative. As moral beings, we are thus those unholy wills that desire to transgress an imperative, for which transgression no pain or punishment can ever atone.

Lacan thus proposes that we read Kant along with his French contemporary, the Marquis de Sade. In the emergence of *libertinage*, he finds something for which Christianity would have prepared the way: the discovery that there is something "unnatural" about our desire, our eros, that is irreducible to our "natural" self-love, or the love or our own good, and the passions and compassions that follow from it. Sade invented a great erotics on the endless demonstration of this truth.

And it is just this truth, just this "eroticism" of the "unnatural" law of our desire that recurs in Freud's account of the way we gratify ourselves in obedience to the voice of conscience: Freud patterns his account of the relation between super-ego and ego on the relation between sadist and victim, or masochist and master. Moral conscience and sadism are both possibilities of a single basic structure that finds in desire something "unnatural" or prior to any good. Thus the sadist has so strong a super-ego that he identifies with it, finding his ego outside in his victim. And, conversely, what "moralizes" the sadism of the super-ego are the processes of internalization and "de-sexualization" through which it becomes attached to standards, and comes to be exercised as though from within. That is why the sadism and masochism that the neurotic shows in his symptoms would provide a demonstration of how we gratify ourselves, beyond our self-interest, in our submission to the voice of duty. And more generally, Freud finds that there is masochistic gratification in the "selflessness" of charity and forgiveness, as there is sadistic gratification in pity or compassion for the sufferings of others.

It is thus our eros that makes of us obligated sorts of beings prior to our observance or transgression of any particular obligation. And, conversely, our eros, our desire, confronts us as an imperative or necessity we cannot locate in ourselves or in the world of our interests. The reason we cannot find it within or without, the reason for its "sublime" transcendence to us, is that it is structured by repression. "The law *is* repressed desire," declares Lacan.

This, for Lacan, is the basic principle of Freud's larger picture of the place of the institution of morality in modern society. A civilization that would base itself in an abstract "law" of duty, liberated from any "pathology," is a civilization that unleashes this other law, which is the symptom of our eros in it. "The *gourmandise* through which [Freud] characterizes the superego is structural, not the effect of civilization, but discontent [symptom] in civilization."[37]

The primary repression, the repression that is "structural" to civilization, or is symptom in it, is thus not an interdiction that happens to fall upon the natural inclinations we might represent to ourselves as hypothetical imperatives. Rather it determines in a "categorical" manner how our eros figures in our embodied libidinal existence. Thus, we don't just happen to internalize paternal interdictions or figures of interdiction: "That (to paint a picture) castration is due to what Daddy brandishes over his brat playing with his wee-wee—'We'll cut it off, no kidding, if you do that again.' "[38] Structural *refoulement* is prior to such familial or social *répression*.

Refoulement is the necessity, beyond any prudential calculation, that says we must, that we can never stop, applying interdictions to ourselves; it structures the manner in which we do so, and the way we gratify ourselves through it. Through interdictions and figures of interdiction we come to present to ourselves and one another this "primordial" fact that we are constituted in our response to the law of our own desire. Thus our idealized identities as moral beings are built up from something in our familial and social existence that we can never fully idealize: our bearings in relation to "the real."

"Morality" as distinct from prudence or instrumentality would thus be categorical necessity before it is rational principle. That is why Kant's attempt to make the two coincide, or have the voice of conscience ask us to do only what, as rational beings, we must anyway agree to do, cannot explain how it is that we gratify ourselves in response to this voice. This notoriously well-disciplined Konisbergian bachelor wanted to know of this gratification in our *âmours* only in the idealized form of the exhilaration of a respect released from interest, passion and compassion. For he wanted this gratification to fall within the bounds of reason alone; he did not want to know anything about its *âmoralité*.

From his diagnosis of this "respect" from the standpoint of *âmour*, Freud derived a new sort of ethical concern. He worried that with a civilization that would base itself, or its "regulative ideals," not in a supreme good but rather in the sublimity of an abstract Law, there goes the problem of this "discontent in civilization" that no agreement as to principles alone will ever settle. For beyond the pleasure principle, beyond what we think is good and what we do to secure it, there in fact lies an aggressivity and a death instinct which recur in the cruelties of our moral conscience and its categorical commands. That is why rather than a "metaphysics of morals," Freud worried about what he called "the culture of the super-ego": this "culture of death."

In identifying this problem, Freud could no longer adopt the Kantian aim of turning us into noumenal selves, showing one another analogically our moral worth as "ends in ourselves." For freedom in erotic matters is not moral autonomy any more than erotic "servitude" is a matter of submission to a deterministic or lawlike nature. The problem is not that of the "heteronomy" of following our natural inclinations, but rather that the law itself, this *nomos* of our desire, is something *heteros*, something fundamentally "other" in our living which we can't represent or control in advance.

In offering a way of interpreting or judging the relation each of us has, in his or her living, to this "other," Freud raised the question of another sort of erotics than Kantian respect and another sort of obligation than Kantian duty: the obligation we have to ourselves and one another as those *âmoral* beings, the truth of whose eros is "discontent in civilization"; our obligation to what in our desire submits us to our obligations.

Bentham's Utility

Jeremy Bentham announced another way to replace and to redefine the ancient ethical philosophies of prudence and *eudaimonia*. Instead of "transcending" the entire world of the good, he sought to rethink what can be known to be "good" in it, discovering in its empirical or natural history a principle and a new means to secure it for ourselves. This new conception of the good, and the kind of knowledge we have of it, is what Lacan admired in Bentham's philosophy:

> If there was something that aired out a bit all this Greek treading-of-water surrounding eudaimonism it was definitely the discovery of utilitarianis. . . . [U]tilitarianism does not mean anything else than this: the old words, those that already served, it is that for which they served, which had to be thought.[39]

In Bentham's idea of the good, the rationality of pain, or the relation between pain and moral reason, receives a new conception. On the one hand, it is not that the immoral man is ignorant of a harm he is doing himself, but that he can be brought to see clearly this his pleasure in his immorality will not pay off. On the other hand, it is not that there exists a great transcendent law of duty to which, independently of all experience, rational agents would come to assent; it is rather that our experience itself may be so ordered by our reason as to obtain what is best for the greatest number. Thus, pain is rational not because the reason of our duty requires the sacrifices of our unholy wills, and not because it is rooted in a prudential ignorance, but because it can be used to better or improve us—it can be used to get us to do just what we ought to do.

Bentham thus had little use for the sort of moral asceticism whose eros Lacan detects in the Kantian "respect" for the law: the real worth of this asceticism amounts only to its utility, and nothing but, and on Bentham's accounting, that was not enough.

There was nothing "transcendental" about Bentham's new principle of utility, nothing "symbolic" or "analogical" about the way it governs our actions. On the contrary, the moral vocabulary that refers to such transcendence or makes use of such symbols, must be reinterpreted. This is illustrated by a central topic in Bentham's thought: the topic of punishment. Bentham thought that the symbolic cruelties of analogical punishments (of the type "an eye for an eye") were inefficient and gratuitous. Thus we should replace the public violence of such punishments with the efficiency of enclosed rehabilitory ones. That was the great thesis of his *Panopticon*; and it is well to recall that the principle of utilitarian morals was formulated in the course of a great unwieldy project to reform the penal code. The *Introduction to Principles of Morals and Legislation* shows his preoccupation with a minute and detailed rethinking of law and punishment: ten volumes were projected.

Central to Bentham's reform in our very conception of ethics is this replacement of a transcendent law and its symbolism with the more efficient work of a natural one. In this light, he proposed to reexamine our old ideas and words of sympathy, compassion and self-sacrifice, and to reinterpret our old political fables of a divine or natural right. In law as in morals, Bentham was indefatigable in his argument that it is much more efficient to govern through a knowledge of the good that really motivates people than through an appeal to principles upon which they would have to agree irrespective of what they might naturally want. It was a time when doctors and civil servants started their long dispute with jurists over the knowledge of that to which law and morals should apply. Such was the "civilization" of utilitarian morals: the one that would no longer have any use for the "fiction" of a supreme Legislator or Judge of which Kant dreamt, the one that would govern through empirical knowledge alone.

Lacan's portrait of Bentham's utility is about the part our eros would have in this new and more efficient type of civilization, and in the new kinds of knowledge it brought with it. If it was through a principled refusal of all "pathology" that Kant would free the analogical "fiction" of the moral law, it was through his rejection of just this sort of fiction that Bentham would come to calculate the utility of moral action. For Lacan, these two great opposing principles of modern morals would have a common source in a law of a different kind: the law of the discontents of a libido released from its service to the ends of ancient *eudaimonia*.

Thus Lacan took the central work in Bentham's voluminous writings to be *The Theory of Fictions*. It was this theory that "allowed a great step in taking off from the old stories of universals in which one had been engaged since Plato and Aristotle, which had dragged throughout the entire Middle Ages, and which still smothered Leibniz, to the point where one wonders how he could have been so intelligent."[40] It was Ogden who extracted this work from Bentham's writings in the thirties, and Jakobson who then brought it to Lacan's attention in the fifties. For Lacan, the importance of the work is that it spelled out the logic of Bentham's attempt to rethink that for which our old moral words had served.

In this opuscule, Bentham draws a distinction between "fictions" and "fables." "Fictions" are not illusory, imaginary or misleading things as are "fables": winged horses and unicorns are "fabulous," not "fictions," entities in this new use of old words. In his logic, Bentham dreamt of a complete, fixed and unexceptionable set of linguistic categories referring to the complete world of existing things. Most of our words, he held, refer to fictitious entities—numbers, relations and classes are fictions and so are abstract notions of space and time. The only "real" or non-fictitious referents of all our talk are those "bodies" to which our senses attest. It follows that most of what we say to one another is quite empty or useless; yet some of it can be translated into terms or sentences referring to real bodies through paraphrastic redefinition: fictions as distinct from fables can be redefined by translating the sentences in which they occur into other sentences whose terms refer only to bodies. The rest of what we say, at least as far as our science and our law is concerned, is fabulous waste.

In particular, Bentham held that such terms as "duty," "title," or "power" would remain fabulous unless they were redefined as applying to situations in which one person is punished by another: "without the notion of punishment, no notion could we have of either *right* or *duty*."[41] Thus, he argued that it makes no sense to talk of "rights" except in cases where there exists a law protecting the right through corresponding sanctions.

In as much as it is not wasteful, empty or misleading chatter, all our moral and legal discourse would refer to bodies, their pleasures and pains. As Bentham dreamt of a language reduced to the bare essentials of all and only expressions that can be translated to refer to bodies, so he dreamt of an exhaustive classification of all possible crimes and matching punishments, such that the potential offender might be able, through simple calculation, to discover that crime does not pay. The word "all-encompassing" which Bentham uses to characterize the utility principle in morals captures this ideal mastery that inspired his theory of language as of law. The logical parsimony that would rid language of its fabulous waste corresponded to the scrupulous classification of what, in the sufferings and gratifications of people can be used to improve them.

Thus Bentham's logic was a legislative one, and his legislature a logical one. The great meta-principle was that there should be no waste in language as in law: that is how he would "air out" the preoccupations of ancient *eudaimonia*. Lacan's question is then what our eros had to do with this great enterprise of a "moral hygiene"— at once logical and legal. He approaches it from the standpoint of what he terms *la jouissance*. It may be, he says, that law (*le droit*) is essentially a matter of the division, the distribution and the retribution of "what there is of *jouissance*." But, he adds, "*la jouissance est ce qui ne sert à rien*" (is what is useful for nothing).[42]

The famous principle of utilitarian ethics says that the rightness of any action is determined by the contribution it makes to the happiness of everyone affected by it. But for this principle itself to be useful, there must exist a good way to estimate the consequences of actions (whether by this is meant the actual or the intended consequences or the ones it would be rational to expect). One must have a complete and individualized knowledge of the population to which the principle is applied. And in addition one must also assume that people are governable, that through the application of sanctions they can be got to do everything they ought to do. Thus Bentham declares: "Nature has placed mankind under the governance of two masters, *pain* and *pleasure*. It is for them alone to point out what we ought to do as well as to determine what we shall do."[43]

Utilitarian ethics thus assumes the existence of a particular kind of knowledge about us, a particular way of controlling our behavior. Behind Bentham's principle stands the emergence of a great classifying and enumerating "Baconian" natural history of our customs and habits. Bentham's compendious efforts to tabulate what would serve "the greatest number" would soon be linked to the new activity of assigning numbers to everything that was called "political arithmetic" or "statistics." This collection of numbers may seem to us indiscriminate, as though there were nothing so unimportant that it should not be encompassed by it. But, Ian Hacking argues that it would pay off later in the discovery of an intrinsic "objectivity" of statistical laws independent of any Laplacian determinism.[44] Statistical inference and utilitarian ethics were to become tied to one another, and thus it would be asked whether Bentham's talk of the contribution to the happiness of "everyone" was to be understood as aggregative or distributative, average or total.

The "moral science" of the counting and accounting of our behavior, to which Bentham's logic belonged, would thus help to shape our "fiduciary" societies of calculated risk. It would alter the very idea of what it is to govern people, and for people to govern themselves. And yet it would have its limits, its problems, its opponents. Just as

Bentham's penal reforms were to have other consequences than those his assumptions made obvious to him, so he had notorious difficulties in completing his vast moral and legal catalogue of human utility; the ideal of total mastery seemed ever to elude him.

For Lacan, this failure exposes what might be called the compulsive character of Bentham's interminable cataloguing. Karl Marx called Bentham "the genius of bourgeois stupidity"; and there is a kind of *bêtise* in the supposition that there is nothing in our experience of pleasure and pain that cannot be so classified and tabulated as to improve us. Lacan analyzes it as a *bêtise* about our eros, about this *jouisssance* for which we have no use. He says there is something about our *jouissance* that would make the perpetual failure that drove Bentham's logic ever further a necessary one; it would expose a "despotism" in the principle that we may be brought to do just what we ought to do.

"The Despotism of the Useful" is the title of a study of Bentham's *Panopticon*, written under the influence of Lacan, by Jacques-Alain Miller.[45] For Miller, the "synoptic" all-encompassing character of Bentham's logic is shown in the "panoptic" character of his correctional reform. For, in effect, panoptic establishments were houses to "materialize" Bentham's legal and moral classifications; and conversely, those logical and legal classifications were "prison-houses of language" restricted to the fiction of function. In both instances the principle would be that everything should be put to as many uses as possible, that everything and everybody should be made to serve the maximum number of purposes, without any waste in time or language.

But there is, Miller argues, at least one utility for which this wasteless universe can offer no account: that of the pleasure taken in the principle of utility itself (or in the pain of its absence), namely Bentham's own utility. The pleasure Bentham took in his all-encompassing "fiction" is, for Miller, a pleasure that can't be classified by it: it does not figure in any of the bodily pleasures and pains, of which legal and moral categories would be the non-fabulous fictions, and Panoptic establishments the material realizations. For it comes from a source unthinkable for such categories. The terrible cheerfulness, the indefatigable optimism of the utilitarian reformer would betray a desire to master something he cannot explain: that there exists in our suffering and our gratifications something that cannot be put to use to serve the greatest number, i.e., this "waste" that belongs to our libidinal existence, to our *jouissance*.

This is where, for Lacan, Freud comes in:

> It is nevertheless here that Freud effects a turn of the pendulum (*fait jouer un retour de bascule*). For experience showed him that once the good is thus encompassed, pleasure dries up, and comes from elsewhere, and, in fact, from the fiction that holds up through the will of the symbolic (*provient de la fiction qui tient au gré du symbolique*).[46]

In this practice, Freud discovered that a patient clings to the imperious manifestation of his own desire, which are his symptoms, beyond any reasonable assessment of their utility, beyond anything that can be encompassed in the tabulated world of rewards and punishments. In our *Âmour*, there is thus a *jouissance* that occurs elsewhere in living than in avoiding bodily pain or seeking bodily pleasure. It is shown in those cases where the two masters paradoxically conspire with one another so that we take pleasure in the experience of a pain, or require pain in order to experience pleasure: cases of the guilt or moral masochism that exposes the erotics of our relation to crime and punishment.

It is of this *jouissance* that Lacan says that it is good for nothing. For it is not something we measure or number (*se chiffre*), but only decipher (*se déchiffre*); it is what "never stops writing itself" in our libidinal destinies, or through this "fiction" that derives from the symbolic. Its necessity, the imperious nature of its "writing" is that of the "law of desire"; and in this sense, Lacan remarks, what this law says to us is "*Jouis.*"

Thus Lacan says that the basic aim of Bentham's theory of fictions was to make logical necessity coincide with libidinal necessity: the necessity of pleasure and pain. In this respect it would resemble the Stoic attempt, with the discovery of material implication, to identify logical with practical or ethical necessity. But since *la jouissance* is precisely something we have no use for, since it escapes any attempt to number or measure its role in our living, this attempt is bound to fail. The "despotism" of the attempt to know and control the two masters of our behavior would derive from this basic lack of mastery, this basic impossibility, this "failure" of our *jouissance*.

And in the ethics of the useful there is thus a violence about which this ethics wants to know nothing. It is the violence that is done to everything about our *jouissance* that distinguishes it from our needs, the violence to the "expenditures" or "investments" of our libidinal energy for which there is no "return," no calculated use. Thus Lacan declares that "the old words, those that already served" would basically have served for this: "that there be the *jouissance* that is necessary (*qu'il y ait la jouissance qu'il faut).*"[47]

Utilitarianism would be, as it were, a vast entangled pun on this "*faut*," which can mean "fails" as well as "is necessary," which is pronounced like "*faux*" (false), and which is part of the expression "*faute de*," where "*faute*" connotes fault or lack, as in the expression "*faute de l'autre*," for want of the other. The "translation" would be, roughly, that the *jouissance* necessary for the "fiction" (or falseness) of utility (namely that people be useful or serve for something) is the one that fails them, for it is the one they incur for want of this other (*jouissance*), because of this lack or fault.

It is by reference to the "failing" of our *jouissance* that we would come to *want* to make ourselves "useful" in the Benthamite sense, and so contribute to the happiness of the greatest number. We become capable of serving, or being useful, for something, declares Lacan "for want of (*faute de*) knowing how to *jouir* otherwise than being enjoyed or had (*joui ou joué*), since it is precisely *la jouissance* that we should not have (or should not fail us): *c'est précisément la jouissance qu'il ne faudrait pas.*"[48]

It is because of the existence of this "other satisfaction" that people, particularly in their erotic being or in their *âmours*, should prove so exasperatingly recalcitrant to the efficient calculations of the utilitarian philanthropist: why, in all their "symptoms" they should seem to want something else than what is obvious to the utilitarian should be good for them to do.

To be unable to see this perversity, or to see it just as more inefficient waste, yet good for nothing, is, as it were, the constitutive *bêtise* of utilitarian morals. That is why utilitarian reform could never understand why symbolic bonds of desire, and the sort of violence, crime and aggressivity they carry with them, should be more important to people than the classified utility of their bodily pleasures and pains. It is why Bentham's great project to naturalize and rationalize what makes us governable as corporeal beings after all involved a fabulous asceticism of a type he wouldn't recognize: it requires a "sacrifice" of this *jouissance* we have no use for; this *jouissance* which must be extinguished or "dry up" in the kind of good he sought to encompass. And it is just this asceticism that recurs in the case of his own motivating desire, and the compulsive busywork of the investigations it imposed on him, to help mankind improve itself, telling it how it can be got to do only what it is good for it to do.

In swinging back the pendulum, Freud would thus ask: What causes us to *want* to place ourselves under the measured guidance of the two masters of pleasure and pain? What is the "necessity" in our desire that makes us think *we must* observe the dictates of utility: this *faut*? What, in other words, is the nature of the pleasure we take in the "fiction" of the theory of fictions? "The only thing to point out to the utilitarian is that man, if he still clings to this puppetry (*tient encore à cette marionette*), only takes pleasure in this fiction."[49]

For the stark utilitarian reference to the bodily masters of all our behaviors would appear to Freud as having the consistency of a "fiction"—of an "idealization" of the imperious *jouissance* that is always failing us. Thus the aim of a psychoanalysis would not be the utilitarian one of making us productive or "well-adapted" to the world in which we function. It would rather be about this "failing" in our *âmours*, and in the words we use to tell of them, that would cause us to ever *want* to make ourselves "functional" or "useful for society." As an "ethics of the real," psychoanalysis would not suppose to know what it might be in our pleasure and pain that points out what we should serve for. It is rather the ethics of what Lacan came to call *l'insuque-c'est*: the "unawares-that-it-is," or the "lack-of-success." This is the sort of "impossibility" that the fiction of our utility would betray.

The friendship of the august philosophical master, the respect of the dutiful law-abiding moralist, the utility of the cheerful social engineer—through Lacan's portraits of these great ethical figures we see the lineaments of another kind of erotics: that of analysis itself. For the analyst is neither a wise friend who knows the Good in which one flourishes, nor a supersensible ego who presents to one the imperative of one's obligations, nor an efficient mental hygienist who knows how to rehabilitate one's unproductive or dysfunctional behavior. Thus unlike the ethical ideals that would "center" us by making us wise, autonomous or productive, psychoanalysis places at the heart of experience something that "decenters" us, submitting us to the singularity of our desire, the unpredictable fortune of our *âmours*. It thus raises the question of an erotic bond that would not be based in communality, reciprocity or equality, but in the singular "bearings" each has to the real. Aristotle told of what brings us together as a harmonious purposeful natural species. Kant explained to us that a reflection on our freedom or autonomy requires us to observe a sublime law of mutual respect. Bentham worked out for us how to attain the good of the greatest number through a logical ordering of the pleasures and pains that would govern all our actions. Freud asked rather how we might be brought together not by prudence, abstract duty or calculated utility alone, but in our sharing of the "structure" of repression or the law which each makes his or her own according to the contingencies of his or her fortune—the structure of the "decentered" subject and its response to the real. What sort of "community" or "fraternity" can we have as divided subjects, each responding to the real in the destiny of his or her *âmours*?

For Lacan, the question of such a bond is one that was raised through the problem of "beauty" in living, which accompanies all the changes in the interval between Aristotle and Freud. It is found in the eros of tragic drama, with which ancient philosophy rivalled, and which recurs in the Baroque and in Shakespeare. It informed the eros in Kant's doctrine of the "disinterested" love of the beautiful, which Romanticism, and then Modernism, would explore. It is at issue in the eros of the transgressive beauty that one would seek in the excesses and waste of utilitarian culture.

The question of this bond is the question of a Freudian "aesthetic" inseparable from the Freudian "ethic." For Freud, "beauty" would no longer consist in an "imitation of the Good" (as Aristotle taught); it would no longer be the "symbol of morality" (which Kant took it to be); and it would involve this *jouissance* good for nothing (whose utility Bentham failed to calculate).

What is the strange "value" this beauty has for us, which is not a matter of "quality," or of the formal accord or harmony between form and content? For Lacan, it is the value of *sublimation*: the capacity we have to present to ourselves this *réel* that would lie at the source of the idealizing ethical fictions secreted in the interval between Aristotle and Freud. Sublimation is the possibility "civilization" offers us for something else than the symptoms of our discontent. That is why there is a curious kinship between analytic and aesthetic experience.

The Value of Sublimation

Sublimation is in effect the other face of the exploration Freud pioneered of the roots of the ethical feeling in as much as it imposes itself in the form of interdictions, of moral conscience. It is the face of that exploration which, for any ear at all sensitive, is designated so improperly and so comically in our century—outside the analytic field, I mean—as the "philosophy of values."[50]

Sublimation is "valued" in civilization in a way that would seem quite peculiar to what has been called the "philosophy of values," for in it we satisfy just what we would otherwise satisfy in our symptoms: our imperious desire. Its value is thus not of a good it would be rational or wise for us to pursue. We "invest ourselves" in sublimatory objects in a different way from such goods; we extract from them, says Lacan, a satisfaction that would demand nothing of us. The "value" of sublimation in civilization is thus an "erotic" one: a value for our *âmes* and our *âmours*. Sublimation is thus the face of Freud's exploration of ethics that is turned towards its promise: the promise of a new kind of bond that would bring us together as subjects of the unconscious, the promise of a new erotics.

Sublimation is thus an ethical as well as an aesthetic category. And Lacan proposes that we read the history of art, or of the "aesthetic feeling" together with the history of love, or of *âmour*. There is of course Socrates' famous submission to the vision of the Form of Beauty in the form of a beautiful boy, which is the initiation into philosophy. Another illustration given by Lacan is to be found in troubadour poetry: in some sense we idealize the art-object in just the same way as the troubadour idealized his lady. In our *âmours* we find the same sort of idealization, the same sort of "distance" that we associate with the experience of art, and conversely, in our experience of art we rediscover something of our *âmours*.

It is thus our *âmour* that infuses and troubles the "aesthetic feeling" so often held to have a "civilizing" effect on us. That is what we find in the great discussions of the formal purity, the untouchable self-sufficiency, or the harmonious self-accord of the beautiful object, or the distance that would separate it from our mundane existence, and the aura it would thereby acquire for us—or, what amounts to the same thing, the demand the beautiful object would make on us to renounce or suspend our "interest" in the existence of things. Indeed it may be said that the Kantian doctrine of "disinterest," along with the later Heideggerian reading of it as *Gelassenheit*, goes back to the mystical and Neoplatonic view of our love-affair with God, where "beauty" or "sublimity" has taken the place of "divinity."

Sublimation would be Freud's way of analyzing this love-affair we have with the things we call "art." We would relate to those objects just as we relate to ourselves and one another as love "objects"; we "overvalue" them in the way we "overvalue" those whom, in love, we idealize. Thus they become the objects of our depressions, our guilt, our anxiety and our mourning; they become the sources of the fluctuating Imaginary play of projection and introjection. They become those peculiar uncanny parts of ourselves that always seem other than ourselves: those things in which we die and live again, occasioning in us feelings of omnipotence or dejection. And, in the form of heritage or tradition, they come to confront us as a source of "symbolic debt," or as what is also known as the "anxiety of influence."

In Freud's theoretical or "metapsychological" definition of it, sublimation is a kind of "vicissitude" or "destiny" of the libido. It is a "deviation" from the aims and objects of the basic partial drives, which would be distinguished by this: Unlike the case of the repression that structures our "private" symptoms or compulsions, it acquires a "public" approval, or is introduced into a socially acceptable space. Sublimation is, as it were, the "public space" of this "other satisfaction" whose fatal effects psychoanalysis reads in the intricate pathologies of our lives. Freud associated with it what he called a "secondary value":

through it one could gain fame and fortune out of what others must repress, incurring their envy and jealousy. But this "value" would derive from the "primary" deviation of the sublimatory destiny of the body, a deviation which in fact never stops troubling those to whom such reputation accrues.

Lacan says that this public space of approbation which sublimation creates from our perverse desire is a very odd one. Why should society approve of the objects which we make from the deviations of our libidos, and then credit with a basically useless sense of "elevation"? What is the "value"of that?

> What can society find satisfying in it? . . . Therein lies the problem of sublimation in as much as it is creative of a certain number of forms, of which art is not the only one—and it will be question for us of one art in particular, the literary art, so close for us to the ethical domain.[51]

One must ask, in particular, in what sense the space of sublimation is a "public" one. For, as a libidinal destiny or vicissitude, sublimation is always the destiny of a particular body, whose fortune is not known in advance. "Sublimation," declares Lacan "is always individual."[52] And what makes a sublimation "public" is not something that reduces or eliminates this singularity. The public of sublimation is not, in this sense, a public of a common denominator, or communality. Sublimation is rather the public space in which our singular perverse bodies may make contact with one another through the creation of beautiful objects that stand for them, without thereby abolishing what makes them singular. It is just for this reason that it creates a public unlike the ones in which people are brought together in pursuit of a common purpose or good, and in identification with a common ideal. Sublimation involves another sort of "bond" among us.

Central to Lacan's account of what makes this bond an amorous one is a theme that recurs in all the literature of love: the theme of the "loss of the object." Psychoanalysis would take a radical view of this loss: our *histoires* are constituted through a fundamental sort of loss, which exceeds our representations of it, and which becomes "forgotten" in the symptomatic manner in which we live. Loss for psychoanalysis is thus event and fortune. It is only in the hazards of finding it again, after the fact, that loss becomes what it is for us. Thus, in finding "substitutes" for the lost maternal object, we would not be replacing something we could otherwise represent to ourselves. Rather it is only by coming across such "substitutions" in our lives that we realize what it has meant for us to have lost it. That is why, according to Lacan, we are always demanding in love more than any "proof of love" can afford, and why to love is to give something we do not possess.

Sometimes putting it into German (*Das Ding*), Lacan gives the name *La Chose, The Thing*, to what it is in our loss that we never possess or represent, but repeat in our *histoires*. He then defines sublimation as "the elevation of an object to the status of The Thing."[53] Sublimation would not *represent* this Thing lost in our *âmours*; it would "recreate" the *vide* left by this loss, which is structurally "unrepresentable" for us. Through this recreation, the loss of the object would discover another fate than those of anxiety or depression, perversion or neurosis.

As an illustration of this definition of sublimation, Lacan takes a saying of Pablo Picasso: "I do not seek, I find." Artistic or sublimatory "creation" is to find again this thing one was not looking for; it is to come across again for the first time something that one was not intending to find. It is the "surprise" of what we were not looking for, and so has the same effect on us a good analytic interpretation. Thus, if our "creations" disclose something about us, it is not a truth we were seeking: a truth about "intentions" we might know about independently of them. Rather, our creations must surprise us, and so come to singularize or individualize us in a different way from the goods we more or less rationally undertake to acquire and consume. Each of us must "find again," must be surprised to find again, what he or she has lost, must thus find a style or idiom that is closer and more precious to one than anything one wants, "intends" or can possess. Sublimation is the public space in which these singular idioms or styles encounter and intersect with one another. That is what we love in it, that is what we value it for.

The ancient idea of *poesis* would then offer only a restricted conception of our sublimations; for our "creations" do not "imitate," do not express or represent, something that could be known to be already there "before" them. According to Lacan, a better model is to be found in the Judaic and later Christian story of God creating the world out of nothing, from which our notion of "creativity" derives. He says that God's judgment on the seventh day, when he rested and contemplated his work of the previous days was, in effect, an instance of divine sublimation. Or, at least, it would be, were it the case that God's satisfaction with himself on this day of "vacation" derived from the "vacancy" or *vide* from which he started out. God would be a "Creator" in the Freudian sense Lacan gives to the term, if this *vide* were that of the Thing, or the lost object. Then his sense of omnipotence—of having creating things once and for all—would be the symptom of the unfathomable desire that provoked him to create the world in the first place.

The reason we value and even "overvalue" sublimation is that in such creation, civilization permits a satisfaction of this *réel* which is incommensurate with the "value" of our ideals or our goods. It is in this light that Lacan proposes to analyze the "fine arts": those arts that would be "fine" or "beautiful" in themselves, and not simply in what they represent. The "radical" or "sublimatory" function of such art would reside in the way we love it, and so find it "beautiful." It would explain, for example, not just why a particular painting is beautiful, but why painting is. In painting we would love what remains "invisible" in the visions it offers us; in architecture what is "uninhabitable" in the habitations it makes for us; in literature what is "unsayable" in what it says to us. Each art would then find a way to recreate the *vide* of our *âmours*.

Thus, in the Seminar on Ethics, Lacan says that apart from the functional purposes of buildings, there would be in architecture beauty or sublimity; through the guises of religion or ideology, our monuments and dwellings would address us and involve us as erotic beings, as *âmes*. The sublimation, which would distinguish architecture from mere building, would lie in the relation of our experience of built space to what it is in our eros that is fundamentally *unheimlich*: what in our eros is at odds with our *ethos* or our manner of "dwelling" in the world. Archictecture is the attempt to enclose or encompass the space of this *vide* in our dwelling as in a temple. And it would then be on the walls of this temple of our sublimation that, as it were, our paintings would figure.

It is several years later, in his Seminar on the Four Fundamental

Concepts, that Lacan advances the famous thesis that the "value" or "radical function" of painting is the sublimation of our experience of "the gaze" regarded as *objet a*. Lacan argues that "the gaze" is the same sort of "object" as are the breast or feces in the psychoanalytic conception of them; and it can be, in its own way, as devouring or expulsive as these more familiar *objets a*. The gaze is thus an *objet* whose fate in our *âmours* we can never represent or know in advance; it is the object before which we would never stop giving ourselves to be seen. Or, put in another way, the gaze is the "tuchical cause" of the fortune of seeing and being seen in our lives, and thus of the regard and self-regard that enjoys such an important place in our ethics, but whose eros is revealed in pathological form in the paranoia of being observed or watched, in the defiant theatrics of hysteria, and in the perversions of voyeurism and exhibitionism.

The "radical function" of painting would be to recreate for us the space of this object: to find again this space which, in Picasso's words, we were not looking for, and indeed, which we can never see as such, since it is always *it* that is looking at us. Sublimation in painting is the art of the surprise that makes visible to us the function of this "gaze" that remains invisible in the great passion of our self-envisagements. We would, as it were, elevate the canvas to the status of this Thing, and, in contemplating or "beholding" a *tableau*, what would "hold" us and fascinate us would be this "annihilation" characteristic of the loss of self in our *âmours*, with its attendant mania, melancholia and mourning.

In the Seminar on Ethics, however, it is the question of the "literary art" that is particularly important for Lacan—this art "so close for us to the ethical domain." It is perhaps in this art that we best see that there is more to ethics than the "values" of the philosophy of values, more than the philosophical "fictions" of what would be good for us. And the literary art that, for Lacan, would first stage the irreconcilability between "beauty" in living and the philosopher's Good is the art of tragedy. Thus the promise of Freud's exploration of the ethical feeling, and of the face of it that is sublimation, would rediscover this ancient art. And the tragedy that best shows the essence of tragedy is, for Lacan, that of Antigone.

Antigone

One sense of the proposition that psychoanalysis has a "tragic essence" is that it is itself *mortal*: it knows itself to have a finite or fatal history. In his polemics with the I. P. A., Lacan underscored this "mortality": the "School" of Psychoanalysis should have none of the ecclesiastical ambitions of a church, whose "group psychology" Freud had analyzed.

It is in the retrospective light of this mortality that we may understand the kind of heroism which, in 1959, at a heroic moment of his own history, Lacan attributed to Freud and to his great "revolution in ethics." It was then that Lacan declared that psychoanalysis has a tragic essence; it was then that he was fascinated by the figure of Antigone, fascinated by her in the same way he says the chorus was, by the *éclat* of her beauty, the beauty of a fatal passion, an "inhuman" heroism, at once fearless and pitiless.

Throughout the many changes in his career, Lacan was fascinated by a series of feminine figures, to which Antigone may be said to belong. At first there was the "erotomania" of the crime of the patient he called *Aimée* (the Loved One), and the Papin sisters, the servants who decided one day to slice up their bourgeois employers, producing a great *affaire* that was to capture the imagination of the surrealists. Later there would be the lady of the troubadours, this untouchable *maîtresse*. And by the time Lacan got to *Encore*, in 1972, there would be the mystic and her *jaculations*: these cries of an enigmatic and imperious *jouissance* one would experience knowing nothing about it. Lacan decided his own *écrits* were of the same order as these cries, as this *jouissance* of which one can know only that one experiences it. At the time of Charcot, one would have tried to reduce such *jouissance* to sex, to *affaires de foutre*. But for Lacan, it was just the opposite. One had only to look at Bernini's Baroque alterpiece representing the passion of Saint Teresa—this Maranos Jewess whose conversion to Christianity would discover an unnameable ecstasy—he said, to see that something else was involved: "this face of the Other, this face of God, as supported by the feminine *jouissance*."[54] "I believe," he declared "in the *jouissance* of the woman in as much as it is *en plus*."[55]

And in Lacan's account of the "origins of psychoanalysis," starting in the circle of Charcot, it is, again, feminine figures who play the crucial role. Indeed "the hysteric" would be the woman who taught Freud about the unconscious, setting him off on the path of the new nonidealistic ethic of what one hysteric named "the talking cure." Later there would be the great question Freud only succeeded in formulating: What does the woman want? Lacan took this to be the question of the central and unresolved problem in psychoanalysis of the "feminine Oedipal Complex," or the relation of "the woman" or of "femininity" to the necessity or structural law of desire. He argued that because of the determinant role of the "desire of the Mother," this question would not be avoided in the conception and analysis of the "masculine" Oedipal Complex Freud had delineated. And so, in Sophoclean tragedy, it was Antigone rather than her father who captured Lacan's attention.

For, in the fascination the feminine figures exerted over Lacan, and according to Lacan, over Freud, there would lie something which the tragedy of Antigone's death would dramatize: the possibility of a feminine beauty and heroism that would come from this *en plus* than that for which men serve, this excess beyond what society holds to be good for us, this Thing held in *souffrance* in what we are or may become. Thus, there would be something *fatal* about the *femmes* that held the psychoanalyst in fascination; and it is in reference to this fatality that the practice of analysis would assume its "tragic essence."

If there is a tragic heroism in Freud's revolution in ethics, or in the new figure of "the analyst" whose peculiar eros Lacan sought at once to define and assume, it may thus be said to reside in this: Freud did not recoil from his fascination with this fatal feminine beauty; he did not seek to evade, to ignore or to repress it. He struggled with it; he sought to analyze it; he tried to provide for a new kind of bond in which it would have a part. We may find this preoccupation in the heroic "self-analysis" he conducted in correspondence with Robert Fliess, the nose-doctor of bisexuality. Could there be a bond of love in which this fatal "femininity" would have another fate than repression, or in which the truth of this *en plus*, about which we can know nothing, might find a way to be said or articulated? Could there be a passionate bond in truth—and in this sense a new kind of ethical *philia*—that would include the question of "femininity," and therefore, of this necessity in our *âmours* we can neither possess nor master? A whole revolution in ethics would be required to even formulate the question: What does the woman want?

It was thus at a heroic moment of his own Seminar that Lacan was fascinated by Antigone as the heroine of a tragedy whose "essence" Freud would have rediscovered in the heart of our modern scientific civilization. In Sophocles' play, he saw the drama of the incommensurability between Antigone's passion and the law of the city, with its supposed good or justice, upheld by Creon. Thus *Antigone* was not for Lacan what it had been for Hegel: the drama of a conflict or contradiction between the spheres of the city and the household, which would be resolved at "the end of history," or in the modern state. It was rather the drama of an irreconcilable *tort* or wrong, and the inhuman beauty of Antigone's self-sacrificial response to it. Thus, still very much under the spell of Kojève, Lacan declared that just at the moment in which Hegel thought that the work of History was coming to its end, "the divergence *éclate* [bursts open] between the individual and the city, between the individual and the State."[56] It would fall to Freud to analyze another kind of "disorder" in history: "another dimension than those of the disorders of the State and the problems of hierarchy. . . . [H]e was dealing directly with the powers of life in as much as they open onto those of death; he was dealing directly with the powers of life that flow from the knowledge of good and evil."[57] For Lacan, Antigone's tragedy was that of this "other dimension," and that is why, he remarks, Anouilh was not so wrong to restage *Antigone* as a kind of allegory of Fascism. For the sort of violence in the city or state which Antigone's fate exposes is one for which there can be no end in history: it is the immemorial violence of what always remains "forgotten" in our historical memory.

In Lacan's vision of the play, Creon becomes the figure of the *bêtise* that lies in placing our faith in a Good men can know. What in the play is called Creon's "error" would consist in the confidence he had in a Good that is, or could be, integrally embodied in *Dike*, the justice of the city and of its written laws. Thus, when, on the basis of the "universalizable maxim" that one cannot equally honor a traitor and a hero, Creon forbids Polynice a funeral, he shows us that "the good cannot reign over all without there appearing an excess about whose fatal consequences tragedy warns us."[58]

Antigone is by contrast a figure whose passion, whose world, is that of death and the "powers of life." Her life is surrounded by death. There is the death of Oedipus, her father, which leaves her abandoned; and Lacan remarks that the Chorus refers to her as *la gosse*, the kid (*he païs*). There are the deaths of her two brothers that set the tragedy on its course; and Antigone, the kid, becomes the figure of the impossibility of mourning. And finally there is her own death, what Lacan calls "the second death." Antigone's death is her own in the precise sense that it is her own concerted action that leads to it. In becoming the heroine of the drama, Antigone will become this "so-voluntary victim," who preferred to die than to live in the city of Creon. Her fateful passion followed another law, another sort of law, one that cannot be written, and of which no man may be said to possess the knowledge. Thus, Antigone's heroism was not at all the "philosopher's virtue," the heroism of the Good we may know, as when Socrates defines courage as knowing what one is entitled to fear. On the contrary, Antigone is fearless as she is pitiless in the intransigence she shows to her sister Ismena: an intransigence which the Chorus recognizes as like that of her father.

If there is something "inhuman," something "inflexible," in what Antigone must do, if there is something *atroce* about her *Ate*, it is that she willingly commits and accepts the punishment for a crime which brings the very "legality" of the City itself into question, exposing its unintended and irreconcilable violence. In assuming the fatal consequences of an act for which the city provides no "image of virtue," no Good to "imitate," Antigone, this willing victim, would discover what, in our passions, Sade would later call the unnatural "crime."

The *éclat* of Antigone's beauty would lie in this incommensurability between the unwritten law of her passion and the written law of the city. It is this *éclat*, over which the Chorus would lose its head in rapt fascination, that would be the source of the famous "catharsis of fear and pity" which Aristotle would take to be the *telos* of a tragedy. The "beauty" of the excess of Antigone's unnatural crime would thus be the "essence" of catharsis, and so of tragedy itself. And it is this "essence" that Freud would rediscover centuries later, in much altered circumstances, connecting it to sublimation, or to the surprise of Beauty in our fatal *âmours*.

"Catharsis" was of course a term employed in the early treatment of hysteria by Freud and Breuer. It referred to the flushing-out or "abreaction" of the unresolved passion that would have its roots in those "reminiscences" from which the hysteric would suffer. In the early drama of the "talking cure," there was this sort of "purgation" of something that had remained in suspense, *en souffrance*, in the passion of the hysteric, writing itself out in the enigmatic bodily symptoms of which she complained, and for which she demanded a cure.

Dora, Irma, Anna and the others would thus become the Antigones of this Viennese theatre without a chorus that transpired in the relative privacy of Freud's office, where the psychoanalyst was to see reenacted the story of Oedipus. In this theatre, Freud focused on the "desire" these hysterics defied their doctors to locate in their bodies, and so to "cure": a desire that he would be brought to recognize was as inflexible, as fearless and pitiless, as that of Antigone herself.

There seems little doubt that Freud was fascinated by this desire and drawn into a great struggle with its curious intransigence. The dream that opens his semi-autobiographical work, *The Interpretation of Dreams*, is about this fascination and this intransigence. Why does Irma persist in refusing the "solution" to her troubled passion, as sure as the chemical formula of a drug? And there is the story of the great travails of his unsuccessful analysis of Dora. When this recalcitrant hysteric broke off her treatment, Freud was forced to review his "solution," discovering something unanalyzed in the interpretation that had sought to link Dora's symptoms to the male figures of her story, and thus to himself—something one might say is closer to the story of Antigone, the kid, than to that of the father who abandoned her. Such was the story Freud told of his discovery of his own "counter-transference," of his own fascination with this desire, for which he had so ambitiously and heroically tried to find the solution.

With this little drama of the failure of his interpretative battle with the hysteric, we may perhaps see the turn through which psychoanalysis was to assume its tragic or "pessimistic" cast. For the more Freud struggled with this desire, and with his fascination with it, the more he came to think that its resistance to analysis was an inherent feature of it: he came to see just how "impossible" the task is of "making the unconscious conscious." He came to think that there is in desire something incommensurate with the knowledge of what is good or bad for us, something beyond the workings of the pleasure and reality principles: an instinct of death. Thus, in the so-called "negative therapeutic reaction," a patient shows that he or she will cling to the troublesome satisfaction of his or her symptoms beyond anything analysis may reveal. The basic "lack of success" shown in Freud's struggle with Dora is to be found in all of his dramatic case studies.

In the intransigence with which the desire of the hysteric had confronted him, Freud would thus find a law or a necessity which, as in the case of Antigone, cannot be reconciled with the good of the city, of the family or of society. He then sought an ethical bond that would include this necessity, or embody its "tragic essence": a bond based on a truth the knowledge of which no one, not even, or especially, the analyst would be the master. Freud's revolution in ethics in this sense would be the one which, cognizant of the fatal consequences of Creon's *bêtise*, would extend a hand to Antigone, this abandoned kid. Such would be its promise: a new sort of ethical bond in which, unlike *philia* or *caritas*, the tragic *ananke* of our desire would not have to be "idealized."

For, the analytic or philosophical passion that would no longer need to rationalize or idealize what is impossible or "uneducatable" in our desire, would be the one that would no longer need to evade the question of the "feminine" face of our *jouissance*: this *en plus*. In such a passion, feminine "beauty" would become something else than this "masquerade" that always conceals what it reveals to men. It would become the beauty of this troubled, *unheimlich* eros in all our ethos, whose truth is "discontent in civilization." And thus the "catharsis" of our unresolved passions in analysis would discover the beauty of "sublimation" Lacan would find in ancient tragedy.

Psychoanalysis would recreate *le réel* in one's history, would bring one to the point of beauty or surprise of a fate one did not realize was one's own. It would open the possibility of "crossing the line" of one's discontents to an unchartered voyage: the singular art of a "sublimation." "The discourse I say is analytic is the social bond determined by an analysis. It deserves to be raised to the heights of the most fundamental bonds that remain for us in activity."⁵⁹ In providing for this excess that "the woman wants," or in extending a hand to Antigone, this social bond would be "tragic" in another sense: it would not be "progressivist." For this bond, the existence of evil would be more, or else, than the absence of the Good, which, as in the case of Creon, men think they can know. Thus, in his Seminar on Ethics, Lacan was at pains to insist that Freud placed no faith in the Victorian idea of the "progress" of civilization, nor, therefore, in the Marxist hope for a "revolution of the proletariat." The desire for such a revolution is at bottom a desire for a master who would know what is good for us. It is as such that this hope would succeed in our century in so mobilizing our *âmours*. But, in passages italicized in the transcription, Lacan declares the problem of evil—of *le mal*—is not even worth raising so long as we cling to this hope for a "progress" that would eliminate its very possibility. As long as we assume that there exists before us "a good to dictate to man his duties," Lacan said, evil will retain "all its revolutionary force."⁶⁰

Our world is not, and will never be, so constructed as to protect us from fortune and secure our good. For our eros has no such "pastoral" state, knows no such "objective" good. No one and nothing, not even ourselves or our society, is to blame for the "violence" of the imperious law of desire in our living and our social arrangements. The ethical problem is rather what we do with this violence, or the bonds we form with ourselves and one another in response to it.

It is in this sense that desire would be the only "ethical universal" we have; and the novelty of Freud's revolutionary practice was to have placed this tragic question at the center of our ethical thought, promising us something new in the possibilities of our *âmours*. Or, as Lacan asked in 1959:

Why does not analysis that has brought such an important change in perspectives about love, putting it at the center of ethical experience, . . . distinct from the manner in which until then it had been situated by moralists and philosophers, . . . why does it not push things further in the direction of the investigation of what must be called, strictly speaking, an erotic?⁶¹

With Saint Teresa taking over the part of Antigone, and the Baroque, the part of ancient tragedy, the drama of Lacan's own story, his own *cheminement*, would lie in his search for what we must, strictly speaking, call a new "erotic." In this pursuit, one may say that Lacan showed himself to be intransigent, to be fearless and pitiless, even "inhuman." Indeed, the tempestuous, and often incestuous, story of Lacan's inability to abide any of the institutions which he founded, or in which he played a part, had a sort of "tragic essence." There came a time when he came to think that psychoanalysis itself, this tragic hero of modern civilization, being mortal, might itself perish and pass away.

Lacan's last years were to be "fatal" years, years of an impasse in the revolution in ethics he had so heroically announced to Gaullist France in 1959, in this *je n'en veux rien savoir* that would have constituted the nobility of his search. How would this "school of the passions of the soul" he had sought so long and at such cost to describe and to institute survive this impasse, this lack of success, this mortality of psychoanalysis? That was the question with which, in his last years, Lacan ended: it was the one he left to us.

It was in this "tragic" or "fatal" moment of Lacan's destiny in French thought and letters that Foucault's project of a new kind of "history of sexuality" would arise. It was then that the question of ethics began to preoccupy him in a new way.

It seems that Foucault wanted to write such a history from very early on, and quite independently of Lacan. In *The Birth of the Clinic*, and later in *The Archeology of Knowledge*, he alludes to earlier versions of the project; and retrospectively one may see its lineaments already in *Madness and Civilization*. But the project was to assume its particular shape in the years of the creative "crisis" Foucault dated around 1975 or 1976: the years Lacan would entitle his Seminar *L'insu-que-c'est* . . .—"unawares-that-it-is" or "the-lack-of-success."

In the new history Foucault formulated during those years, Freud was to have a quite different role from the one he had enjoyed in his previous work, and, in particular, in the last chapters of *The Order of Things*. Freud was not the hero we had thought him to be. He was not this doctor who had opened up a dialogue with madness which several centuries of psychiatric "monologue" had closed off, and who had thus discovered in our psyches the same sort of *absence d'oeuvre* painters and poets had found in our language and vision; he was not this practitioner of the "perilous act" of thought, the contemporary of the "transgressive" philosophy that had rediscovered the work of Sade.

Thus we should no longer take Freud as belonging to the "critical" or "creative" present that renews our thought, but on the contrary, as something *from* which we would be critically departing, something that is receding into the past from which we must distinguish ourselves. We should no longer think of him as the hero, but as a passing figure in the genealogy of our conception of ourselves as sexual beings.

Thus Foucault started to ask: How on earth could we have ever turned something so peculiar to us, and so transitory, as our "desire" or our "sexuality," into a great ethical universal, the source of a modern tragic drama? How could we have asked of it to tell us the truth of our living, our becoming, our *histoires*? How did we ever come to associate it with this enigmatic Law it would take the interminable labors of interpretation to read in our living, how did this imperious "hermeneutic of the self" take hold of our thought and our ethics? What had led us to thus superimpose on our private, internal pathologies the heroism of a great epic or tragedy, and so believe that "beauty" in living—this "aesthetics of existence"—was marked by a "tragic essence," as though the only alternatives to the violence of our existence were brutality, repression or sublimation?

With this questioning Foucault set out on the strange new voyage of his last work. His genealogy of our very ideas of "sexuality" and of "desire" would be a search for a new image of the passion of thought, a new sense of erotic possibilities. And yet, in this philosophical pursuit, Foucault would never lose contact with the problem he thought Lacan was the first to raise in psychoanalysis after Freud: the question of truth, the question of "spirituality."

Part 2
Foucault

It is the same with skepticism in ethics as it is with skepticism else-where, that the more general it is, the more harmless.
—Bernard Williams

Eros After Desire

Foucault focused on truth, on *Wahrsagen*. That is what he admired in Lacan: the ethic of this difficult or "tragic" truth in our libidinal existence that would exceed any knowledge of our Good. Yet to this grand idea, he wanted to address a series of skeptical questions. Did we really have to place at the heart of our eros a "signifying chain" that would always be leading back to an impasse or failing in our desire, and forward to the intricate role this desire would keep having in our lives? Or was this not just the presumption of a specific practice of interpretation, a particular "hermeneutic of the self"? Indeed, could it be that the "revolutionary" idea of ourselves as "subjects of desire" in fact continues a confessional tradition, a *jeu de vérité* of a time and place that had made it possible to say only one sort of truth about ourselves: the truth concerning our "desire"?

Foucault's question was then: Outside the moral idealisms of our good, can we invent no other truths about ourselves, no other passion for truth, no other "game of truth" than the psychoanalytic one? Foucault bet that we could, and that in some sense were already in the process of doing so. Perhaps we were already departing from the thrall of the "desire of the analyst" and the strange dramatic world of its interpretation; perhaps we were in fact no longer content to conceive of ourselves as "subjects of desire"; perhaps indeed in our eros we were no longer Greek, no longer Christian, no longer Freudian, but were becoming something else. What sort of truth-saying might arise in this new erotic situation?—that was what Foucault called "my problem," the problem not of desire but of "truth, *Wahrsagen*, and the relation between it and the forms of reflexivity, the reflexivity of the self over the self."[1]

In his last work Foucault sought a new sort of *Wahrsagen*. How today might we "speak truly" of love and friendship without the nineteenth-century conception of our "sexuality" and its characteristic perversions and deviancies, and without the Freudian "hermeneutic of the self" that tells us that our "desire" is always "written" in whatever we say and do, and that we therefore require the long hours of analysis to "read" it? Foucault's problem about truth was therefore a problem about love and friendship: the problem, in short, of a "new erotic."

To do this Foucault took it upon himself to show that the question of "desire" introduced through the Freudian "revolution in ethics" was not universal, but rather "historical"—a singular and contingent invention we may in fact be able to do without. This was no mean task. It required of Foucault "to recenter my entire study on the genealogy of the desiring man, from classical antiquity through the first centuries to Christianity." For, "in order to understand how the modern individual could experience himself as a subject of a 'sexuality,' it was essential first to determine how, for centuries, Western man had been brought to recognize himself as a subject of desire."[2]

The Freudian "revolution in ethics" had placed us under a basic, even overriding, sort of obligation: to be true or faithful to our desire; concerning our desire we must never deceive ourselves, we must always be honest with ourselves. What sort of duty was this? It was not part of the elaboration or justification of a fixed code of conduct, and was supported by no Cosmology or Moral Republic. Indeed, merely "conventional" or "bourgeois" moral rules stood in the way of it. Rather it singled out in our experience of ourselves something at once recondite and internal. Locked within each of us was an uncivilized desire, and to be honest about it, or faithful to it, would consist in releasing it, in showing and telling of it, in a "game of truth" in which some would become more adept than others.

Foucault's argument is that this "desire" and this duty to expose it, have not always been with us. The famous condition laid down by the Delphic Oracle for those who consulted it was: "Know yourself!" But it is an anachronism to think that this meant "Be faithful to your desire!" How then did this duty to desire arise? When did people start to assume that what is most questionable, and potentially most glorious or heroic about themselves as erotic beings, were not the occasions and distinctive pleasures of their activities, but the "truth" of the fantasies, wishes and thoughts locked deep within the recesses of their minds or souls? How had it become possible to think that being dishonest about desire was the source of a "symptom-formation," a disease, whose cure required that one enter into a discursive game with others? How had the idea of such "self-deception" come to require a great philosophical rethinking of the very idea of consciousness or self? And why had this basic "*méconnaissance*" come to attach itself in a privileged way to sex, or erotic experience?

How, in short, had people been brought to believe that a terrible truth about their sex resided in some inaccessible or "blocked" portion of their psyches, and thus that, in the deepest sense, their sex took place primarily in their heads? For Foucault it was a practical matter. Basic to the duty towards desire and the new game of extracting it and speaking truly of it, was a principle of an "incitement to discourse": ever more sex, ever more truth. In an interview he states what he sees as the result of this practice of incitement: "we moderns have become obsessed with our inner desires; acts don't matter so much to us; and pleasure—nobody knows what it is any longer!"[3]

Foucault argued that our modern obsession with a recondite desire was not so important in antiquity. Primarily it was an invention of Christianity. It is in Christian cultures that sex would start to be linked to an arcane encoding of inner impulses it takes a "hermeneutic of the self" to unriddle. The fundamental contribution Christianity would make would not reside in its code of forbidden and permitted acts, but in the type of experience one was thought to have of oneself as an erotic being.

In Foucault's reconstruction of the ethical discourses of antiquity, what in sex was thought so dangerous or worrisome as to become the object of a whole set of self-transformative practices was not yet the sins of the flesh, or the odd bestial impulses that would fascinate us and lurk in the pathogenic recesses of our heads. It was an excessive activity that threatened a loss of self-possessedness in those meant to rule: a danger for the ethos or appropriate conduct of the free adult man. The ethos of the ancient "civic man" in health, home, and court-ship, around which these practices would turn, was rather different from the ethos of the Christian "inward man," and the Augustinian problem that all of sex is infected by the Fall, and is the model of sin in general.

Foucault's idea was that the conceptions under which sex becomes problematic to a people have varied with the kinds of morality they invent to deal with it. Thus, if what was thought worrisome about sex in antiquity has become somewhat unfamiliar to us, so too has the kind of ethics they devised to treat it: ancient ethics was not a strategy to normalize a population, nor a matter of abstract inner obedience to universalizable rules. How then could one analyze the changing conceptions of the relation between sex and ethics?

Foucault's last books introduce a scheme to analyze this question. He distinguished the question of "ethics" from the question of a moral code. It is one thing to issue an interdiction; another to determine whether people actually obey it. Still another is to invent a way for people to become not simply moral agents, but moral kinds of being or persons. That is what Foucault calls "ethics." Given a more or less explicit set of prescriptions and interdictions—what Foucault calls a moral code—one can examine the practices through which people were incited to acquire a moral nature.

As Foucault uses the terms, "moral" refers to the prescriptive code one is obliged to follow on pain of sanction, internal or external. "Ethical" refers to the kind of person one is supposed to aspire to be, the kind of life one is incited to lead, or the special moral state one is invited to attain. There are thus "moral" problems about the code, its principles and its applications; and then there are "ethical" problems about how to turn oneself into the right kind of person. He then proposes to analyze such ethical problems and their transformations in terms of a fourfold scheme in which there is first an image of the right sort of person or life or soul; then the authority which incites one to attain it; then the means provided to do so; and finally the description under which one's sexual experience becomes relevant for such self-transformation.

Thus, Foucault argues that in antiquity, the description under which erotic experience was placed was that of *aphrodisia*: an interlocking of desire with acts and the pleasures they procured that threatened to undo the proud self-mastery of the free man, sexual pleasure being, in Plato's words, the most keen and frenzied. According to Foucault's analysis, in order to deal with this danger, ancient thought, medical, poetic and philosophical, invented the image of the master, his choice of a true and beautiful style of existence, and the means to attain it.

The intent of this analysis can be seen in contrast to the displacements Christianity would introduce. In Christianity what one would be asked to attain is no longer the proud virility of the master; it is an inner purity of being. What incites one to transform oneself is no longer the choice of a noble existence glorified for posterity; it is the commandment or will of God. Sexuality is thought to be problematic not because of the dangers of an excessive, unhealthy or dignified indulgence, but because the flesh is forever impure. And, it is thus that we find that the dietary, medical, poetic and erotic means the ancients devised to maintain a noble self-possession are replaced by the endless and arduous task of deciphering one's inner thoughts: the temptations, the seductions, the deceptions that the devil has put in our heads. Christianity would thus be the start of the internalization of eros, or the process through which people were led to find their sexuality within themselves. One may recount Foucault's story through the figures of Artemidorus of Daldis, Saint Augustine and Sigmund Freud.

In the second century A.D., Artemidorus wrote a book of dream interpretation which was widely used. It taught how to tell one's fortune by reading one's dreams. In particular, several chapters are devoted to sexual dreams, and Foucault provides an analysis of them. The principle of interpretation he isolates is based on an assumption central, though not specific, to ancient views about sexual experience: the analogy between hierarchical social roles and the positions or roles one assumes in sexual acts—active or passive, on top or on bottom, and so on. It is a conception in which the act of penetration, and thus the male member, is what counts in sexual experience, since it provides it with its social significance. Sexual dreams can then symbolically confirm or reverse proper social relations and so augur well or poorly. Thus the sexual dreams in Artemirodus' book are ones in which someone dreams about himself in a little drama of penetration and passivity or of pleasure and the expenditure of energy, which tells of his fortune.

The meaning of the dream depends on the social status of the dreamer. If, in one's dream one finds oneself in a passive position with an inferior, things don't augur well. If, however, it is with a superior, the dream counts as a favorable sign.

Artemidorus' readings are somewhat unfamiliar to us. If, for example, a man dreams that he has sex with his mother, that means he is likely to succeed as a magistrate, since it is obvious that one's mother is the sign or symbol of one's city or country. In Artemidorus, interpretation of dreams is not focused on the nature of the sexual act but on the social or civic status of the partners: sex is relational, and relations of sex are indissociable from relations of status.

In Saint Augustine we would find another conception or ourselves as sexual beings. Foucault draws attention to the passages where Augustine offers a description of the sexual act as a sort of horrendous spasm: the whole body is shaken by a terrible jerking in which one loses possession of oneself, and, in particular, of one's capacity for deliberation. This description is not new; it is virtually a transcription from the pagan literature of the previous century. But Augustine inserts it into a new context; he was apparently one of the first Church Fathers to admit that sex could have taken place in Paradise before the Fall. Sex in Paradise could not, of course, have had the horrible epileptic form that it has unfortunately assumed for us (or for us men). Before the Fall, the body, and each part of it, was wholly obedient to Adam's *will*, and sex occurred as though a hand that gently sows seeds in the earth.

But, as we know, Adam rose up against Good with the pride or arrogance of acquiring a will of his own; and in losing the support of the Word of God he lost his paradisiac possession of himself: his body, and its parts, were no longer obedient to the commands of his will. They revolted against him, and the sexual parts were the first to "rise up" in disobedience. Adam's shame was this loss of his will over his body; that is why the famous fig leaf was said to conceal an erection. Sex in erection is the image of man's revolt against God: the pride or arrogance of sex is the punishment and the consequence of the pride or arrogance of man. His uncontrollable sex is to him what he has been to God, a rebel who rises up in revolt.

Augustine gives the name "libido" to the rebellious or autonomous movement of the male organs. The strength, force, origins and effects of the libido become a central problem that confronts man's will. But the libido is not an external obstacle to the will; it is a sort of worm that eats at it from within. That is why the struggle against the assertions of the libido requires that one turn in on oneself; that is why it requires not simply a mastery of one's activities and relations with others, but a diagnosis of the illusions and deceptions, the thoughts and desires, in the most secret recesses of one's soul; that is why it requires a permanent or unending hermeneutics of desire—unending since one's will and one's libido can never be substantially dissociated one from the other.

Foucault goes on to analyze how such techniques for one's self-scrutiny as a libidinal being were introduced, elaborated and transformed in the monastic context; and then how they came to be spread far and wide through the agency of the Christian pastoral.

If we now look back to Artemidorus, we might say that the crucial question of sexual ethics has passed from the problem of penetration and relations with others to the problem of erection and one's relation with oneself, or more precisely, of one's will to the involuntary assertions of one's libido. We are still quite obviously concerned with male sexuality; but the male organ—or "the phallus" as it is now sometimes fondly called—is no longer the proud organ of activity through which a man affirms his civic status; it has become the mark of a primordial passivity that strikes to the core of a man's inner will. And, to overcome this passivity it is no longer sufficient to turn one's eyes upward to recall the eternal truth one has forgotten; one must continually turn one's eyes downward and inward to decipher among the movements of the soul those that arise from the libido. It is no longer a question of the appropriate or healthy occasions for sexual activity, but of the inner purity of sexual thoughts and desires.

And, if the light of faith is required for this permanent obligation to track down impure thoughts, it is also the case that one can have no access to the truth without the purification of the soul. Foucault thinks we need to wait until the curious sort of spiritual exercises that were Descartes' *Meditations* to find a path to truth based not on purification, but simply on the self-certainty or evidence of representations themselves.

But now what of Freud? Like Artemidorus, Freud wrote a highly influential book of dream interpretation. *The Interpretation of Dreams* is one of the great works of the hermeneutics of desire of our time. It is also a confessional work of sorts—that is one thing that links it to Augustine. For it is Freud's own dreams that are at issue; it is the book of the famous self-analysis that led Freud to the truth he asserts in the last chapter of the book: that desire is the essence or core of our being.

It is therefore astonishing that, unlike Artemidorus, in Freud's book, we find no *sexual* dreams at all. It is rather non-sexual dreams which tell of hidden sexual desires. The principle of interpretation has changed: meaning no longer depends on the social status of the dreamer, but on the intricate web of associations that link his dream to his innermost desire. Where Artemidorus told us how to pass from sexual dreams to our fortune in civic life, Freud told us how to pass from our non-sexual dreams to the truth of our inner being.

In a footnote Freud explains why he included no sexual dreams in his book. It is not that they are shameful or an improper topic of scientific investigation. Freud says he finds it laughable that, in the German translation of Artemidorus, the chapters on sexual dreams were censored. The reason he offers for not including sexual dreams is rather what he calls "the still unresolved problems of perversion and bisexuality."[4]

What was important in such dreams for Freud was thus not, as with Artemidorus, what they tell about the fortune of a man with a particular "position," but what they tell about a dreamer's deep sexual nature, his bisexuality or perversion. In this respect they are no different from non-sexual dreams. But, if Foucault is right, such a concept of bisexuality was completely foreign to the conception of sexual experience embodied in Artemidorus' book. It was just assumed that men might actually pursue partners of both sexes. But nobody referred this fact to a deep bisexual nature or tendency. By contrast what Freud called a bisexual nature or constitution typically belonged to a person who did *not* pursue both sexes, who did not have a sexual practice or activity with both sexes. In ancient conception where such activity was taken for granted, it occurred to no one to imagine that outside of it, a person might harbor within himself a hidden bisexual or perverse constitution.

For such reasons one might say that the internalization of desire has assumed a new form: sexuality becomes a truth about desires buried in a childhood we refuse to recognize but which returns in our neurotic symptoms. Desire is still what is most questionable and most glorious about us; it still harbors a truth we have the obligation to tell. But that obligation is no longer commanded by the will of God but by the norms of mental health; and the authority on which it is based is no longer a theology of the flesh but a science of sexuality.

This story of Artemidorus, Augustine and Freud illustrates something of the plot of Foucault's story, of his attempt to account for how we ever came to conceive of ourselves as subjects of desire. There is the problem of penetration and status; there is the problem of libido and will; there is the problem of desire and mental illness. They belong to different ethical worlds, different possibilities of life. And as the description of sexuality passes from one to another, we observe a great process of transformation and internalization in our conceptions of ourselves as ethical beings.

It was Foucault's view that our own ethical predicament today would be to rid ourselves of this long internalization through which we came to think of ourselves as "subjects of desire." He thought that our times were marked by a new dissatisfaction, a new refusal, a new "problematization" in our conception of our erotic being and its possibilities: we would want another kind of "erotic subjectivity" than the ones based on the virile model of penetration and status, the Christian model of sin and confession, and the therapeutic model of hidden emotion and cure. And so we would want a new kind of ethic whose principles would not be derived from the demands of the super-ego, the will of God, or the requirements of a normal development.

It was in relation to Time or History that Foucault sought this new type of *Wahrsagen*. Sex would no longer be a matter of the cosmological time of the opportune moment, the *kairos* of sex in one's life and the noble memories one leaves of it. It would no longer be a matter of the eschatological or Augustinian ages of history in which we should at last be delivered of the terrible thorn in our flesh. It would no longer be a matter of the normal maturation or development in social forms. It would rather become a question of deforming, resisting, departing from what our history presents to us as timeless, as universal, as given about who we are and may be: a matter of undoing, complicating and opening up the forces of our erotic fatality.

Contemporary sex liberation movements provided Foucault with a site for this opening and rethinking of eros. What he found important in them was the way eros and ethics were together departing from the categories of "sexuality" and the assumptions of the inner truth of desire. Thus, in 1976, he declared:

> The real strength of the women's liberation movement is not that of having laid claim to the specificity of their sexuality and the rights pertaining to it, but that they have actually departed from the discourse conducted within the apparatuses of sexuality. The American homosexual movements make that challenge their starting-point. Like women, they begin to look for new forms of community, co-existence, pleasure.[5]

The American movement was important for Foucault himself; he referred to what he called "the laboratories of sexual experimentation in San Francisco and New York."[6] His research, subjective and archival, into the history of sexuality, would coincide with a time, which, in the words of David Halperin "would seem in retrospect to have been the high-water mark of the recent political movement for lesbian and gay freedom in the United States,"[7] where, of course, Lacanian psychoanalysis had little impact.

In these "laboratories," Foucault discovered that the kinds of relations men may have with one another were being opened up in new ways. In particular, gay men "have to invent from A to Z a relationship that is still formless, which is friendship: that is to say the sum of everything through which they can give pleasure to one another."[8] In this site not yet governed by law, rule or habit, what empassioned Foucault was this "still improbable" invention of new relationships. "What relations, through homosexuality, can be established, invented, multiplied and modulated?"[9] For Foucault this was a very different sort of ethical question than "Who am I?" or "What is the secret of my desire?" Rather than a "form of desire," here, at least, homosexuality was taken to be "something desirable." It was "an historic occasion to reopen affective and relational virtualities," through the "diagonal line" it would trace in "the social fabric."[10] For,

To imagine a sexual act that doesn't conform to law or nature is not what disturbs people. But that individuals are beginning to love one another— there's the problem. . . . Institutional codes can't validate these relations. . . .These relations short-circuit it and introduce love where there's supposed to be only law, rule or habit.[11]

In particular we should see S/M in this light: not as an intrinsic "deviancy" rooted in infancy, of which the neurotic would dream in horror, but as a precise experimental game people choose to play in order to discover new "virtualities" and augment the singularity and intensities of their pleasures. It serves to alleviate the sense of boredom when the sexual act becomes too available; it serves to attenuate the assumption that all "passivity" is demeaning, as in the "macho" preoccupations of ancient pederasty, which Foucault found so distateful.

Something of the eros of Foucault's detailed analysis of the techniques of punishment in *Discipline and Punish* is to be found in this "pragmatic" focus on just how things are done. And the feature of contemporary gay literature that captured Foucault's curiosity was the explicitness and precision of its descriptions of the body and its activities. He thought that this great precision came from a form of living in which the anonymous encounter had replaced the lengthy rituals of courtship and seduction. It was a kind of erotic practice in which activity comes first and "spirituality" after. As such this literature, and the form of life from which it derived, would be a rather different sort of thing from a sublimation.

The basic idea of sublimation is that there exists something so terrible about our desire that we must articulate it in "cultural" forms, and not directly through erotic practices. Sublimatory "spirituality" would be the response "civilization" offers to the endless trouble our perverse desire introduces into our living. In effect, in his last research, Foucault turned this idea around: it is only the strange conception we have of our "desire" that induces us to believe that we gratify it in a more fundamental way through the beautiful forms that recreate it than through the "perverse" activities, apparently so much closer to it, which, left to themselves, would end in violence, brutality and death. For Freud the question of sublimation had been: What relation must the subject have to his own "desire" for him to satisfy it through creations very distant from sexual activity? Foucault asked instead: What peculiar notion of our desire must we have to think that we must dissociate it from our erotic activities and "reinvest" it in objects? Thus Foucault declared:

> What strikes me is the fact that in our society art has become something which is related only to objects, and not to individuals, or to life. That art is something specialized, which is done only by experts who are artists. But couldn't everyone's life become a work of art? Why should the lamp or the house be an art object, but not life?[12]

Even in the case of artists we may observe that the singularity of their creations belongs to the invention of singular ways of living. In contrast to Sartre, accordingly,

> we should not have to refer the creative activity of someone to the kind of relation he has to himself, but should rather relate the kind of relation he has to himself to a creative activity.[13]

In this way "beauty" would count as an important ethical category in how we might live.

The question of the "creative activity" of one's free formation of oneself was, of course, a very old one: the role of eros in the beauty of living was already raised in the time of Socrates and Alcibiades, rather independently of the question of art-objects. Indeed in Foucault's reconstruction, it was the choice of a noble existence, and not an abstract law, that supplied the motivation for ancient ethical practices. In the "historic occasion" opened up by the liberation movements and their laboratories, Foucault thought that this question, and this sort of motivation, might again form part of our ethics and our eros.

In his last research, Foucault sought a new "erotic" after Desire. He wanted to restore to eros its sense of improbability, innovation, the beauty of unguided "experimentation." To do this would be to put behind us the great psychoanalytic theatre of an arcane libido; the "truth" of our eros need not be thought to have this "tragic essence." For "desire" is not prior to history, but only one of its singular inventions. Thus, for the "fatality" of our libidinal existence, we should substitute the "determination" of the historical forms through which we become "subjects" of our erotic experience. Our history is not the memory of an immemorial violence we have forgotten; it is rather what determines and delimits who we can be through specific forms, from which we may nevertheless depart.

"Who we are" at a given time and place, while historically "determined" is yet never historically "necessitated." Our freedom lies in the contingency of our historical determination; and thus to our existence always belongs the possibility of "new forms of community, co-existence, pleasure . . ." To reinvent ethical thought today, asking again the ancient question of how to speak truly of our lives, became for Foucault a matter of understanding how our bonds, our freedom and our truth might form part of a contemporary critical philosophical activity.

Bonds

Community was a central question in Foucault's ethic: it was about the bonds we may have with one another, affective and political; it was about who we are and may be. In stressing "subjectivity" and "subjectivization" he did not intend to abandon a social or collective ethic in favor of an individual or private one. Rather, he wanted to rethink the great question of "community": the question of how and why people band together, of how and why they are bound to one another; the question of the passion or eros of our identity.

Foucault held that the answer to this question was not to be sought in a single generic "nature," sociological, theological or philosophical. For our "subjectivity" is in fact given to us through many "dispersed," contingent and changing "systems of thought"—bodies of discourse and practice that enable us to identify ourselves both as individuals and as collectivities. Foucault's formulation of the question of bonds was this:

> In what way do individual and collective experiences arise from singular forms of thought? that is, from what constitutes the subject in relation to the true, to rules, to itself?[14]

Behind these "singular forms of thought" there would be no single monolithic human nature. Foucault advanced no "theory of the sub-

100 TRUTH AND EROS

ject," and did his best not to suppose one. Rather, in the manner of Wittgenstein's attempt to divide up the unity of what is called "the mind" or "the mental" into a loose array of public language-practices, Foucault sought to analyze the many and various things people must say and do to themselves and each other in order to identify themselves, and so play their parts in "forms of life." There would be an irreducible and changing "multiplicity" of such forms, with no single origin or source. To say that such forms of thought are "singular" is to say that they are "contingent." That was a basic assumption of Foucault's ethic. Identificatory forms of thought are not inevitable or necessary but rather change, undergoing transformations, becoming the objects of contestation and struggle, and confronting other or new ones. "Forms of thought" have a complex history, which is the object of no one's planning, and which often goes unrecognized.

Thus we do not have to see the ancient ethical question of how best to live as either an individual or a collective matter. It is rather a question of the kinds of individuality and of collectivity of which we are capable at a time and place, and of the relations they suppose with particular sorts of government and self-governments, knowledge and self-knowledge.

In the nineteenth century there had arisen the great dream of a *Gemeinschaft* that would be prior to the social divisions and bureaucratic rule of modern states. In it would reign a harmonious division of goods and tasks, a natural equilibrium of force and authority, and a stable source for the identity of its members. How, it was demanded, might such Community be regained? Superimposed on labor struggles and urban discontents, Community thus became the source of a critique of the individualism, the privatism, the alienation, the atomism and the anomie of modern societies. Our modern individuality would be the dissolution of a great Community we must fight to regain. How might we live again beyond private property, the monogamous family, or urban uprootedness?

In this more or less Romantic sense of the term, Foucault was no "communautarian." The search for an essentially good or conflict-free communal existence struck him as having had disastrous consequences. He questioned that there had ever existed such community, and held that the critique of contemporary society did not depend on it.

The critical side of Foucault's thought was rather directed to the "naturalness" through which "systems of thought" maintain their hold over us: there is nothing given or natural about our membership in social groups, and we must ask "how [do] we recognize ourselves as a society, as part of a social entity, as part of a nation or state?"[15] Similarly there is nothing given or natural about our "individuality," and we must ask how we come to recognize ourselves as individuals.

Our "subjectivity" is not an "individuality," an indivisible unit in which we locate our identity; and it is not "particularity" or the exemplification of a common nature. It is not a single thing, and there are as many "subjectivities" as there are accepted forms of self-relation. Each of us can have more than one kind of subjectivity, more than one kind of social being. Thus, individual and social being are not opposed to one another as absolute entities, one requiring the dissolution of the other. Instead they are linked together in a common his-tory, the forms of one being able to survive a change in the forms of the other. Thus, they are not the givens of critical analysis, but just what requires it. Foucault's critical question was not the presence or absence of Community taken as a good in itself, but the kinds of community we may have with one another.

We may distinguish three kinds or senses of "community" or "bond" in Foucault's critical philosophy. First there is *given community*. It consists in the possible relations to ourselves and one another that a particular system of recognition makes available to us. It is the kind of community people *think* they have with one another. This thinking is rooted in an institutional or "material existence." But that doesn't mean that it is determined or confronts us as an insuperable force; rather it shows what one is up against, should one attempt to contest or change it. For, in the second place, there is *tacit community*. The ways people devise to identify themselves are supported by their own activity. They must be willing to do their bit in maintaining the systems that define and delimit them; they must play their parts in a "game" whose intelligibility and limits they take for granted. The tacit community of a system of recognition is everything people must do to maintain its hold over them. But this hold does not reduce to the force of arms or to ideological mystification; it resides in the force or authority of its very self-evidence. "Given community" is accepted or tolerated because one cannot see what else is possible. Thus, to accept it is more than to find it just or legitimate, and to find it unacceptable or intolerable is more than to find it unjust, even if the exposures of its hidden injustices can help make it so.

In the third place, when a system of identification is found unacceptable, there is *critical community*. The possibility of critical community comes when the interruption, refusal or reversal of forms of given community leads to the exposure of the tacit community which supports it. Thus, Foucault maintained that "resistance" has an analytic role, related to a truth: it exposes what a particular strategy of "power" is. It discloses something unseen and unacceptable in a form of identification, and exposes it to risk. Critical community is thus the result of a "problematization" or "crisis" in the self-evidence of a community of a time and place. It is the sort of community or bond we may have in so far as we are free.

In short, given community arises from an identification: "I am an X." Tacit community is the materially-rooted system of thought that makes X a possible object of identification; and critical community sees this system of thought as singular or contingent, finds something "intolerable" about it, and starts to refuse to participate in it. It is the community that "problematizes" identity and thus makes of our "subjectivity" an open and endless question, at once individual and collective.

Foucault tried to characterize such critical community in terms of the tradition that had linked the activity of "the intellectual" to philosophy. The nineteenth century had invented the "cosmopolitan" intellectual, defined in contrast to all "particularisms." But what Foucault called the "specific intellectual" was not a "particularist" one, delimited by a regional, national, ethnic, religious, or sexual identity. On the contrary, it was the one who starts to see such "particularity" only as historical "specificity," or who questions the thinking that secures such "particular" identities.

He then tried to insert such "specific" critical activity into the great post-Kantian philosophical tradition of historically-minded critique. This would require the following changes: the "community" of critical philosophy would separate itself from the assumptions of a transcendental subjectivity, either individual or collective. And the aim of critical thought for such a community would not be to fix the universal or legitimate bounds of all possible experience, but to open experience to new possibilities. "The point, in brief, is to transform the critique conducted in the form of a necessary limitation into a practical critique that takes the form of a possible transgression."[16] Thus, the "critical community" of Foucault's ethic was not a "transcendental" one, but the community of the specific moments of critical "transcendence" in the forms which make a particular kind of "subjectivity" possible.

Accordingly, the "responsibility" of critical philosophy would have to be redefined. It would not be the paternalistic responsibility of ancient civic virtue. It would not be the liberal responsibility towards an "individuality" prior to social identity. It would not be the historical responsibility for the new Socialist Man.

In what would its passion consists? What would motivate it or inform it? What would be its relation to truth, or its "spirituality"? In it Eros would not play its traditional part of binding us together into an essential community, discovering a natural harmony or equilibrium with one another. For "critical community" is a community of struggle with its own historically constituted identity; its violence, and so also its "beauty" and passion would be of a particular sort.

Gilles Deleuze says of Foucault that he was the contemporary philosopher most free of the preoccupations of the last century. And that is why those preoccupations were such a constant object in his critical histories. In particular, Foucault was concerned with the failure of the progressive ideologies or critical theories of the nineteenth century to understand and to confront the specific kind of racism that was to explode in the twentieth.

Our twentieth-century problem is not *Gemeinschaft*; it is "identity," the sort of identity shown in the spectacular irruption of racism and nationalism. We may view the opposition between "individualism" and "collectivism" in nineteenth-century philosophy in terms of their attempts to overcome or eliminate the problem of "particularist" identity.

Thus there was a model of the new socialist or communist man, transcending all religious or ethnic identities in a great historical mission. And then there was a rival model, reactivating old ideas of contract or natural right, of an "individuality" that would be prior to all particular cutlural or communal identities, as in the situation of the individuals in John Rawls' "original position." Both models could appeal to the progressive "cosmopolitan" sentiments of intellectuals; they could see racial or national identity as only an "imaginary" form superimposed on a real prior individuality or social being. Thus it would be thought that nationalism and racism had no "real" existence, but were rather "ideological" atavisms to be explained in terms of the progressive march of history to eliminate, or to restrict, the State, and install "liberalism" or "socialism."

With his *The History of Sexuality*, Foucault was working with another picture: the twentieth century was in fact rooted in a very "real" but singular or specific sort of identification and exclusion, central to forms of government the War did not eliminate, and with which we are not yet done. Instead of seeing the grand nineteenth-century philosophies of Man and Society as the only alternatives to this "technology" of government, we should analyze these philosophies in terms of their critical response to it, or the way they effected internal modifications in it. The name Foucault gave to this modern strategy of government was "biopower." It had arisen in the seventeenth century with new forms of the administration of the internal and external policies of a state that were directed to the "life" of its population.

The central category was the great complex idea of norm and normality. "Normality" was not an abstract legal principle of the entitlement to govern; it was not a prudential principle of wise authority, or a way of insuring our insertion in traditional holistic communities; it was based neither in contract nor status. It was rather a way of identifying us, and of getting us to identify ourselves in such a way as to make us governable. It was a "singular form of thought" from which individual and collective experience arose. It did not at all oppose individual and collective experience, and its central problem was not the conflict between the individual and society. On the contrary, the more "totalizing" the reach of its administration of the life of society, the more "individualizing" the nature of its identification of us became. One may observe that where the workings of this type of governmental thinking were securely implanted, there has never been a modern revolution. It was then in relation to this new concrete manner of securing our identity as individuals and as part of states that Foucault proposed to rethink the nineteenth-century philosophies of liberalism and socialism.

In particular, he argued that the capital invention of "political economy" was not that of the "ideology" that would be exposed by Marx. It was rather the proposal of an internal self-restriction on the operations of bio-political administration made in the name of a greater efficiency in securing its goals. Thus, we should not think its categories of "civil society" or "the people" were universal entities lying outside any "state." We should rather analyze how they figured in the very historical or specific "system of thought" on which the effective experience of government rested.

With his analysis of "normalization," Foucault refined a central theme that runs throughout his reflections on community: the problem of exclusion. His histories were directed to those whom a society deprives of acceptable discourse, or excludes from its self-definition. It would seem that exclusion has always been part of the philosophical attempts to define what makes us part of communities. Athenian citizenship supposed the exclusion of slaves; and modern citizenship is bound to the exclusions of the nation-state. This was, in some sense, Foucault's starting point. At first he held a sacrificial or exclusionary view of what constitutes identity in society.

> Traditional sociology, sociology of the Durkheim type presented the problem in this way: how can a society hold individuals together? what is the form of the relation, of symbolic or affective communication, that is established among individuals? I was interested by the somewhat opposite problem, or, if you will, by the opposite response to the problem, which is: through what system of exclusion, by eliminating whom, by creating what division, through what game of negation and rejection, can a society begin to function?[17]

Thus, we would identify ourselves as good, normal, rational people only by excluding from ourselves, our society or our acceptable discourse, what we take to be abnormal, irrational or dangerous about ourselves.

But when he came to think of the workings of "power" as not fundamentally "negative" or "repressive," but "positive" or "formative," Foucault qualified his view of systems of identification. He sought to distinguish the struggle of "critical community" from any Romantic identification with who or what a society would exclude in order to constitute itself. Rather its critique would lie in those moments when such workings of a society, together with its characteristic techniques of exclusion, begins to erode, to lose its self-evident hold and become "problematized." The "technology" of exclusion, or the rites of sacrifice, belong only to a particular system of thought and discourse, or are an inherent feature of it. Thus, the punishment of a regicide is a very different thing from the anonymous rehabilitation of an offender. "Being a criminal" is defined in a different way, the first questioning the rule of the Sovereign, the second disturbing the functioning of Society. It is one thing to identify with the passion of the delinquent; another to question the form of thinking that defines what delinquency is, and the role it has in society: the role of "critical community." Thus, more generally, "critical community" is not the community of those a society excludes in order to function, but of all those who start to refuse their part in maintaining the specific form of thinking that defines it and them, of those who depart from it, taking their identities or forms of experience in new directions outside its compass.

In *The History of Sexuality*, Foucault argues that the racism of our century rested on specific economic and political policies. And in those policies, "sexuality" played a particular role: there was a great fear of an aberrant or degenerate sexual activity and being, of another pathological kind of satisfaction, threatening the existence of society from within and without. The panic, the loathing, the murderous anxiety characteristic of the passion of national or racial purity and superiority was thus linked to notions of sex. Foucault argues that this passion was formed through a particular way of thinking, through particular racial and national techniques of identification and exclusion, and the types of knowledge on which they relied. Central to this manner of thinking was the partially "scientific" category of *degeneracy*. The category was not all foreign to socialist thought. Indeed, Foucault declares:

Modern antisemitism began in that form. The new forces of antisemitism developed in socialist milieus, out of the theory of degeneracy. It was said that Jews are necessarily degenerates, first because they are rich, secondly because they intermarry. They have totally aberrant sexual and religious practices, so it is they who are the carriers of degeneracy in our societies. One encounters this in socialist literature down to the Dreyfus affair.[18]

Thus, the terrible specificity of "modern" anti-Semitism in the history of racisms would lie in the attempt on the part of a nation-state to systematically eliminate the "degenerate" portion of its own "population."

In the project Foucault outlined in *The History of Sexuality*, the basic conjecture was that if "sexuality" had become important to our identity in so many ways, it is because its construction or institution belongs to the history that implanted "normalizing" ways of government and self-government. It was under this heading that it would come to be thought to be an intrinsic property of our individual and our social being; and it would be as such that it would be connected to "degeneracy." The nineteenth-century invention of "sexuality" would form part of the history that gave to the great anxiety about degeneracy in modern life its sexual coloring. The new sexual science would help link the fear to the "perverts" and "deviants," who threatened the cohesion of society, and whose myriad forms it catalogued, analyzed, and sought to cure. Psychoanalysis would have an important but ambivalent part in this process.

Foucault is the first to make the whole question of degeneracy central to a history or an "archeology" of psychoanalysis. The political honor of Freud, he says, lies in his theoretical refusal of the notion of a natural sexual degeneracy. And yet what he found to oppose to it was an "archaic" or primitive "desire" connected to older ideas of symbolic Law or Sovereignty. Against the category of the Norm of Society, Freud reintroduced a theory of the Law of Civilization, and its discontents.

For Foucault, psychoanalysis would still postulate a source of identity that would not be "historical" in his sense: a source that would be prior to history, or which would see history itself as a response and a repression of its violence. It still had a "theory of the subject" as distinct from a "history of subjectivizations," a theory that says that who we are is determined by an order or a fatality which, if it is not familial, would be "symbolic." This would be the "archaic" or mythical element in Freud, the nineteenth-century face of his thought, tied to the "tragic" theme of the origins of civilization which he expressed through a fictive anthropology or prehistory of the "primal"—just the features of Freud's thought which Lacan reinterpreted in terms of "structure," in terms of the ontological or primordial "fact" of desire and its law.

As against such erotic archaism, Foucault argued that "we must conceptualize the deployment of sexuality on the basis of the techniques of power that are contemporary with it."[19] In particular it would be a sort of "retroversion" to analyze the passion of modern fascism, with its "fantasies of blood" and its "paroxysms of disciplinary power" in terms of some great "crime" that would found civilization. Rather, Foucault thought we should make the historical construction of identity and the passion of identification the central issue. Instead of seeing "desire" as the great "other" of social, political or ethical relations, we should see it as only one element in the history that constructs the possible forms of such relations. Instead of analyzing our identities as "forms of desire," or as responses to the archaic or primordial "fact" of our desire, we should open the question of what we think is desirable about them.

Thus, Foucault thought that the limitation of psychoanalysis was shown in its inability to imagine a passionate mode of being in which the whole category of degeneracy would have no part, as it had not in ancient ethical thought and practice. Foucault wrote that Deleuze and Guatarri's *Anti-Oedipus* was a sort of manual for a "non-fascist way of life." And he himself sought a kind of eros, a type or critical passion, that would be non-racist, or anti-racist, in the particular sense that identity would not be the source of self-assertion and exclusion but the target of a questioning through which people might start to depart from the historical limits of their identifications, taking their particularities as so many historical specificities.

It is in this context that people might ask what is "desirable" about their mode of existence (and what not) rather than asking what form of Desire it expresses. In this passion they might then rediscover the old theme of the "beauty" of a free existence. Such beauty would no longer be thought to lie in a discovery of a harmony with a pre-existent transcendent order, but would rather consist in trying for form oneself just where there arises a "critical transcendence" in our historically given forms of identity, just when the art of living frees itself from "rule, law or habit."

We may think of Baudelaire as a nineteenth-century figure already concerned with this question. His "ironic heroism of the present" would find no place in existing instituted social relations, but would transpire "in another different place, which Baudelaire called art."[20] For Baudelaire, the sort of urban "anomie" against which nineteenth-century sociology recoiled in horror, searching for the security of a holistic Community, would become instead the source of a great unnatural or artificial beauty in living: the beauty not of a metaphysical harmony, dwelling or *Heimat*, but of a "still improbable" identity. Baudelaire may have thought of this search as a sort of archaism, as a "sublimation" of archaic impulses. Perhaps today, Foucault thought, we might take up again this question of the "beautiful life" in terms of the bonds of a critical experience not limited to what Baudelaire had called "art." We might think of it in terms of "critical community" and the kind of freedom that it experiences.

Freedom

The moments of critical "problematization" within the history that constitutes us were, for Foucault, times when our thought and our being is "freed" for new and uncharted spaces and possibilities. In this sense "critical community" is a "free community" and the passion of the critical "bond" a passion of being free. As such it would continue the ancient ethical theme according to which the art of leading a noble or beautiful life was an art of being, or of making oneself, free. "The critical function of philosophy up to a certain point emerges right from the Socratic imperative: . . . ground yourself in freedom through the mastery of self."[21] But in taking up the idea of freedom, Foucault sought to rethink it: our freedom would not lie in our essence but in our historically contingent singularity.

In this sense, the experience of freedom would not be an experience of an identity or a natural or pregiven state, but, on the contrary, an experience of the fragility of a kind of identification taken for granted. Who we are would not be the image or source of this freedom, but just what is constantly freed or opened to question by it. Thus, it is not in our basic individualities or communities that we are free; it is rather the historical forms of our individual and communal being themselves which must be freed or exposed to the risk of new and unforeseen transformations.

Foucault held that there are as many kinds of freedom possible as there are such historical systems of identification and servitude. There is no such thing as freedom in general. The "subject" of freedom varies with the specific techniques people devise in relation to their history to make themselves free; a "free subject" can mean many different things.

> I don't think there is actually a sovereign, founding subject, a universal form of subject that one could find everywhere. . . . I think on the contrary that the subject is constituted through practices of subjection, or, in a more anonymous way, through practices of liberation, of freedom, as in Antiquity, starting of course from a certain number of rules, styles and conventions that are found in the culture.[22]

The "common stakes," he declared of historical analysis and political critique, are that "we are not, and do not have to place ourselves under the sign of a unique necessity."[23] For Foucault, freedom and determinism in history were not mutually exclusive. Freedom is not the absence of historical determination or fatality, and historical fatality is not the absence of freedom. For freedom is not "in" history as a great general image of an ideal state confronted with the brute necessity of nature. It is rather a "condition" of the history that delimits our being, and it always works itself out as a history: the history of the specific things people do to themselves and their world to make themselves free.

The *existence* of freedom (that we are not under the sign of a unique necessity) resides in the fact that no historical determination of our being is absolute, that any such determination is exposed to events that interrupt it, transform it, and reinterpret what it is. The *experience* of freedom is an experience of such an event that frees our relation to the practices and the thinking that have historically limited our experience. And the *practices* of freedom are what people try to make of themselves when they experience the existence of freedom in the history that has formed them. At the juncture of historical analysis and political critique would thus lie the task of "freeing" this experience in the history of our "subjections," asking what then might specifically be done to make ourselves anew.

For Foucault freedom was thus not a *state* one achieves once and for all, but a condition of an "undefined work" of thought, action, and self-invention. As such he tried to introduce it into politics and ethics. To be free, he argued, we must be able to question the ways our own history defines us. In his idiom, to the degree that a system of thought or government seeks to rule out this possibility, it is a form of "domination." Foucault's principle was that no form of power is ever completely "dominating" in this sense. The history of a kind of power is never such as to in fact exclude altogether that people will question it, revolt against it, organize to overthrow it. Thus, if there is no society without some kind of power, there is none whose power is total or absolute. Freedom is therefore not the end of all power, but an inherent limit of its continuing exercise:

> there is no face to face confrontation of power and freedom which is mutually exclusive (freedom disappears whenever power is exercised); ... rather than speaking of an essential freedom, it would be better to speak of an "agonism," ... a permanent provocation.[24]

It follows that freeing ourselves or liberating ourselves is never total or absolute either. "I don't think there is anything that is functionally— by its very nature—absolutely liberating."[25] Freedom always remains still to be done, and we are never done with it. Its basis is not to be found in anything a cosmology, theology, psychology, or legality says we are; rather we must place such theories back into the primary practical context through which they concretely affect us. For that is the only guarantee our freedom can have.

> Freedom is a *practice*; ... the freedom of men is never assured by the laws and institutions that are intended to guarantee them. That is why almost all of these laws and institutions are quite capable of being turned around. Not because they are ambiguous, but simply because "freedom" is what must be exercised. ... I think it can never be inherent in the structure of things to guarantee the exercise of freedom. The guarantee of freedom is freedom.[26]

To be free is thus to be able to question politics, to question the way power is exercised, disputing its claims to domination. Such questioning involves our *ethos*, our ways of being or becoming who we are. Freedom is thus an "ethical" matter. "Freedom," Foucault declares, "is the ontological condition of ethics; but ethics is the deliberate form assumed by freedom."[27] If the existence of freedom in history conditions the elaboration of an ethics, that ethics is the attempt to endow this existence with a specific practical form.

Kant is the modern philosopher to make of freedom a "condition" of the very possibility of ethics or morality. He helped to introduce into ethics the task of freely "constructing" or "making" ourselves in a free space not governed by the necessity of nature, or based in a natural knowledge. But by inserting the question of identity into the heart of such critical philosophy, Foucault departs from the complex Kantian distinction between laws of freedom and laws of nature. For Foucault, the experience of freedom is not the experience of a law or principle. The "condition" of freedom does not stand to its "deliberate forms" as a general regularity to the cases it subsumes; it is not a "regulative ideal" one must instantiate or exemplify. It is rather the condition of the "undefined work" that opens new possibilities for being, and that exposes the presumed "necessity" of inherited ones. That is why a critical philosophy of freedom "will not deduce from the form of what we are what it is impossible for us to do and to know, but it will separate out, from the contingency that has made us what we are, the possibility of no longer being, doing or thinking what we are, do, or think."[28]

This idea of freedom, as an "ontological condition," however, was not the dream of an experience of freedom released from all "technology." On the contrary, Foucault stressed the techniques or practices of freedom. He wanted to rethink *techne*, making the question of freedom a "technological" one, a question of "technologies of the self." Foucault held that what counts as "free action" or "free being" is always action or being under a particular sort of description; he then argued that such descriptions acquire their intelligibility through concrete practices or "deliberate forms." Thus, one may say that as an "ontological condition" freedom never prescribes the descriptions under which our actions must fall, but rather "frees" us with respect to those descriptions. The experience of freedom never tells us *what* we must do; that is just the job of the "practices of freedom." Critical philosophy is then the attempt to specify what it is about ourselves and our world that must be freed, and what we must thus do to make ourselves free. That is why freedom always remains a practical or "technological" matter.

In particular, Foucault hoped to introduce this practical question into modern liberation struggles.

> I've always been a little distrustful of the general theme of liberation, to the extent that . . . there is the danger that it will refer back to the idea that there does exist a nature or human foundation which, as a result of a certain number of historical, social or economic processes, found itself concealed, alienated or imprisoned in and by some repressive mechanism. . . . [For], when a colonial people tries to free itself of its colonizer, that is truly an act of liberation, in the strict sense of the word. But as we also know, that in this extremely precise example, this act of liberation is not sufficient to establish the practices of liberty that later on will be necessary for this people, this society and these individuals to decide upon receivable and acceptable forms of their existence or political society. That is why I insist on the practices of freedom.[29]

Freedom is thus not the end of a liberation struggle, but the condition from which it derives and the question it poses. "Liberation" is not a state in which all possibility of domination has been eliminated, but the critical opening of new ways of determining what is tolerable or acceptable in the manner in which politics is conducted, and lives led. For in struggles against oppression, or in favor of rights, people cease to tolerate their complicity in a form of power; it is then that the existence of freedom occurs in their history, and the question of the practices of freedom is posed for them.

Sexual liberation struggles are a case in point. Foucault sought to analyze more concretely just what is "free" about them, just what they serve to "free up" in our historical experience of ourselves. He tried to locate the emergence of a critical space of experience, in which, with respect to passionate or erotic relations, we might ask again what to do to "exercise" our freedom:

does the expression "Let us liberate our sexuality" have a meaning? Isn't the problem rather to try to decide the practices of freedom through which we could determine what is the sexual pleasure and what are our erotic, loving, passionate relations with others? It seems to me that to use this ethical problem of the definition of practices of freedom is more important than the affirmation (and repetitious, at that) that sexuality or desire must be set free.[30]

Thus, "sexual freedom" would not lie in license or in self-control. It would not be a matter of the acts one may or may not perform, or of an autonomy impervious to what happens to one. For, the servitude against which it is directed is the historical limitation of our very conception of our erotic experience, and freedom is what would make that conception something open-ended and improbable. In his last research, Foucault tried to uncover the genealogical sources of this conception of freedom, its condition and its practices.

Freedom or *eleutheria*, he declared, was a central preoccupation in the practice and thought of ancient ethical schools:

in antiquity the will to be a moral subject . . . was principally an effort to affirm one's freedom and to give one's life a certain form in which one could recognize oneself, be recognized by others, and in which posterity would find an example.[31]

Such affirmation of freedom was, however, not open to, or required of, everyone. On the contrary it

concerned only a very small minority among the people and even among those who were free. There were several forms of freedom: the freedom of the chief of state and of the army had nothing to do with that of the sage.[32]

And, indeed today

it is very difficult to know who participated in this morality in Antiquity and under the Empire. We are thus very far from the moral communities schematized by the sociologists and historians who study an assumed average population.[33]

To understand the underlying way of thinking or "tacit community" that allowed this minority to affirm its own freedom, Foucault thought we must thus dispense with "the platitude more or less derived from Hegel" according to which "the individual in ancient society would be submerged in the noble totality of the city."[34] For in fact freedom was then an individual matter, even if not yet an "inward" one. It was part of a "care for oneself," which, in contrast to the "social ethics" to be developed later, was primarily a matter of "self-regarding virtue." Foucault argues that it was the "care for self" which required responsibilities towards others, not those responsibilities that imposed a certain kind of relation on oneself. It was in order to make oneself free, or to affirm one's free being, in a recognizable and exemplary form, that this minority of men came to observe a particular sort of ethic in their relations with one another.

One may regard Foucault's study of the medical, domestic, political and philosophical literature of the period, with its problems of excessive *aphrodisia* and ethical *akrasia*, as an attempt to isolate the "singular form of thought" which made of a man's individual and civic being the source of an affirmation of a virile freedom. Central to this way of thinking was a specific danger to oneself and to the rule of the city, an ignoble servitude. It was not the danger of poverty, unemployment or deviance; it was not the danger of Adamic vanity and original sin. It was the danger of *slavery*, and in particular, slavery to oneself. *Eleutheria* meant basically not being a slave.

Accordingly, *eleutheria* was not conceived in contrast to a natural causality, a statistical regularity, or the will of a God. The noble "self-mastery" of the ethical man was not yet a self-renunciation; "care for oneself" did not yet command a "selfless" or charitable relations to others. Yet this task of affirming a noble *eleutheria* was not a task for slaves, but for the citizen's own relation to himself, and the example he sets for others. "[a] slave has no ethics. Freedom is then in itself political."[35]

Thus, it was as a model or analogy that slavery was important for the ancient practices of freedom. Through this analogy, mastery of oneself would be bound up with a mastery of others in both household and city. One should rule oneself as one should rule a slave. But, to properly rule others, one had first to know how to rule oneself; and it was best for those who could not do so to submit to the wise authority of those who could. Thus, the affirmation of freedom rested on a famous lack of reciprocity; it depended on the existence of those who could not exercise it on their own.

This pattern of thought is found in Plato's famous analogy of the soul and the city. For it was not just that government or *arche* in the soul is like government in the city, and involves analogous parts. It was also that the best city was the one where those who know how to rule themselves are the ones to rule others. And where this *eidos* of the best city is not yet instantiated, it should serve as a model for the relation a man must nevertheless have to himself in order to be free.

In ancient thought, the art of being free was in short an art of mastering oneself in the face of the risks, the abuses, and the excesses of ruling others. But this art, as an art, also came to involve another sort of *maître*: the master who teaches how to be free, what to do to truly master oneself in wise or temperate rule of others. Being free was thus linked to *paideia*, and the forms of knowledge and self-knowledge it required of one; and so it would be linked to the freedom of the sage. It was in this pedagogical context that Plato would argue that to be truly free one must know how to separate appearance from reality, and so contemplate the true or metaphysical nature of the soul.

Foucault presents this "politico-pedagogical" matrix as governing the sorts of "practices of freedom" that were invented from Antiquity to the Empire. The matrix would be undone as the "spiritual" problem of inner freedom came to be separated from the external problem of civic duty of the exercise of political power. Thus, Foucault tried to isolate a basic change in what might be called the "ethical subjectivity" of power, which he formulated in this way. The leader of Plato's *Republic*, he said, had to be a philosopher; later, with Aquinas, it would be enough for a monarch to be virtuous, a just government being the one that imitates God's creation in promoting the *honestas* of man. Machiavelli would still be concerned with how a Prince might reinforce his relations with his subjects. But with the new seventeenth-century science of the administration of the objective population, wealth and territory of a state, a new sort of figure would emerge.

For the first time, the person who was to rule others had to be a "politician"—a figure characterized not by membership in a higher ethical community, but by the knowledge of the "reason of state" with its internal and external policies. The politician would be judged not in terms of his philosophy, his godliness or his *virtú*, but by the efficiency or competence through which he pursued the "policies" of his state. Indeed, an early name for the knowledge or science he practiced was *Polizeiwissenschaft*. And in these "policies" or "policings," the individuals to be governed would no longer be conceived in the ancient manner: "the marginalistic integration of individuals in the State's utility is not obtained in the modern state through the form of ethical community which was characteristic of the Greek city."[36]

In particular, it is through this process that "economy" would cease to mean "the rule of the *oikos*" and the model it offered for wise or "paternalistic" government, and would become the name of an independent reality governed by its own natural laws. The great discovery of "political economy" would be the moment when the knowledge of this reality became central to government. Classical liberalism would emerge as an internal limitation the state would impose on its own policies.

In this modern political context, new practices of freedom were invented. One way the question of freedom would come to be formulated would be this: Which part of one's actions or thoughts are one's own to dispose of as one wills, and which part is one obliged to transfer to the regulation of the State? At first, Foucault sought to define his own view of freedom in contrast to the classical sort of question.

The context for this conception of freedom and the state was a legal one. It is to a "reactualization" of Roman law in the writing of modern constitutions that we would owe what might be called the "property- or ownership-theory" of freedom, power, and their relations to one another. According to this theory, freedom is something we own or possess by nature or by right: it is a "good" we dispose of, and which we may thus together invest in a sovereign authority. The question then becomes to decide the portion of this basic property individuals should be entitled to keep, and the portion they should agree or "contract" to turn over to an independent authority, applicable equally to all of them.

In contrast to this view, Foucault advanced his own conception of power, and of modern forms of power in particular, not as sovereign authority, but as a complex anonymous strategy of rule, with varied sources, and with the consistency of a kind of knowledge or reason. Accordingly, he proposed what might be called a "no-ownership theory" of freedom: the practices of freedom are not something that is owned or belongs to anyone, by nature or by right. Freedom is not just a possession we dispose of and use. To have it we must "exercise" it, and to exercise it is to be able to question a kind of power, or refuse a kind of servitude, in the way we have been constituted. Thus Foucault played on the word "constitution." In reference to Hobbes, he said that instead of thinking of power as "constituted" through agreement among ourselves as owners of freedom, we should think of freedom in terms of the historical process through which we come to "constitute" ourselves as subjects of the sort of activities through which we may be governed and may govern ourselves.

It follows that an historically constituted manner of governing—a form of "power"—does not itself arise from free consent, even if we may seek to restrict or limit its operations through consensual procedures. "Power is not a matter of consent. In itself it is not the renunciation of liberty, the transfer of rights, the power of each and all delegated to a few."[37]

And yet a form of power supposes a tacit acceptance or toleration: people must be willing to do their bit in maintaining it, and that is something they may come to refuse. Thus, while freedom is not an individual possession from whose transference the authority of power derives, it is a "condition" of the history that delimits or "constitutes" individuals in the game of government and self-government in which they participate.

It was then under this conception that Foucault hoped to reintroduce the ancient conception of freedom as *ethos* or concrete way of being, and so to reconnect the "spiritual" and "political" senses of freedom, whose ancient politico-pedagogical identification is no longer possible, credible, or desirable for us.

In questioning the "ownership theory" of liberty propounded in the classical doctrine of sovereignty, Foucault was, of course, hardly alone. One finds objections to it already in Spinoza's quarrels with Hobbes; and one may argue that this Spinozistic tradition would be taken over by Marx. In our time it is continued, among others, by Hannah Arendt, who declared that "the greatest and most dangerous difficulty" confronting our view of freedom, and thus our freedom itself, is the inadequacy of classical "sovereignty-theory."[38]

Arendt brings out a question that was to increasingly preoccupy Foucault in his last years: what it means to *speak* publicly, freely, critically, or the link between the "practices of freedom" and those of critical discourse. The conceptual and practical interconnection between "being free" and "speaking truly" would be the topic of Foucault's last lectures on *parrhesia*, the word which in classical Athens came to be used for "free speech" or "freedom of speech." Among the "events" that would give rise to the invention of the art of philosophy would be a sort of crisis or "problematization" in the practices of speaking freely: in the critical practices of *Wahrsagen*.

As a type of free speaking, *parrhesia* was something more than permitted speech; its "freedom" was more than a right to speak. For a state to permit or allow it is not sufficient for it to exist, just as for a state to seek to suppress it is never enough to eliminate its possibility. Thus, we should not restrict our understanding of it to our own modern constitutional or legal view of the right to free speech. Rather we may take it as "ethical" in the sense Foucault gave to the term: as a matter of how people recognize themselves as "subjects" of free critical discourse, or of what relations to themselves and to one another they must have in order to speak truly about themselves. In this way we may see in ancient *parrhesia* a start of the activity of critical *Wahrsagen* of which Foucault dreamt: the attempt to open an experience of the freedom that conditions our participation in the history that "constitutes" us as individuals, as members of communities, and of states.

Foucault would then formulate the question of free public speech in a different way from Hannah Arendt; his account does not turn on her great distinction between private and public. For Arendt, being free was an intrinsic property of an "original" realm of thought and action. In this realm, "slavery" to the particular interests and necessities of domestic or private life would be overcome or suspended. Only in this way or in this place would being free and speaking truly discover their fundamental or original tie to one another.

Thus, Arendt saw the "sovereignty-theory" advanced by Rousseau and then introduced into critical philosophy by Kant as a dangerous decline from this public realm. The modern conception of a subjective or private "free will" that would precede and cause actions would obscure in a dangerous way its own derivation from the public realm. To be free again we must thus expose the derivative character of the very concept of the free will, rediscovering the primordial sort of "publicness" of which freedom is an intrinsic attribute. For Arendt, the great difficulty and danger of sovereignty-theory was to have removed freedom from the space which gives it its true meaning: it had sought to transpose the concept of freedom from an external, worldly, public activity to a subjective, internal, private state.

Foucault's lectures on *parrhesia* offer another picture. "Free speech," even in Athens, was not fundamentally a speech that transpired in an original realm, dissociated from the slavery or necessity of the *oikos*. Long before the invention of the "free will," *parrhesia* would have both "public" and "private" uses. Indeed part of the "genealogy" of the concept of "free will" is to be found in the elaborations of both public and private parrhesiac activities, in particular in Roman philosophy, which Arendt declares is no philosophy at all. Moreover, not only did the activity of *parrhesia* occur both in private and in public, but the public occurrence of it was not restricted to democratic assemblies. Another political use was in the council or advice given to kings.

The activities of free or critical discourse thus cut across the private/public distinction then as now. And Foucault sought to analyze the "realm" of speaking truly and freely that ancient philosophy defined for itself in another way.

One source for this historical question is the hermeneutical study of A. Momigliano of the term *pharrhesia*.[39] He finds that until Athens of the fifth century, *eleutheria*—the condition of not being a slave—and *parrhesia*—saying whatever one wants without regard for conventional or traditional restrictions on doing so—were not linked to one another. For Homer, *eleutheria* was still conceived in the context of war and conquest.

The Athenian connection between the two was a semantically, as well as a practically, complex one. For unlike *isegoria*, the equality or right to speak in assembly, *parrhesia* was also thought a private virtue: a matter of the way of being, the *ethos*, and even the *eros* of the one who speaks. It is as such that the term occurs in the debates about democracy, notably in the passages of Book IX of the *Republic*, where Plato argues that philosophy and democracy are incompatible, passages to which Foucault draws attention.

According to Momigliano's study, this distinction between *isegoria* and *parrhesia* would recur in the Latin distinction between *libertas* and *licentia*, and eventually in the modern distinction between the "positive" and "negative" conception of freedom. It would come to figure as well in the Christian doctrine of the "truth of conscience" as the *parrhesia* of speaking with God; it would thus have a hand in what Foucault proposed to analyze as "pastoral" discourse.

In his lectures, Foucault hoped to add yet another sense, or to rethink *parrhesia* in yet another way: in terms of the "concern for truth" that would be characteristic of his own ethic, his own passion of free critical community.

> I believe too much in truth not to suppose that there are different truths and different ways of saying it. To be sure, one cannot demand a government to speak the truth, the whole truth, nothing but the truth. On the other hand, it is possible to demand from governments a certain truth as to final aims, a general choice of its tactics, and on a certain number of particular points of its problem; that is *parrhesia* (free speech) of the governed, who can and must summon, in the name of knowledge and their experience and because they are citizens, the government to answer for what it does, the meaning of its actions, and the decisions it has taken.[40]

Truth

What is thought? What is philosophy? According to Gilles Deleuze, these were the questions that haunted Foucault throughout the long labors of his archival research. Foucault rejected as ludicrous (*dérisoire*) an older image of philosophy as a timeless supervenient discourse that would sit in judgment, assessing and fixing the bounds of what is true in all other discourses. Today philosophical "critique" must assume another form.

> There is always something ludicrous in philosophical discourse when it wants, from the outside, to dictate the law to the other discourses, telling

them where their truth is and how to find it, or when it takes upon itself
to inform their development into a naïve positivity; but it is entitled to
explore what, in its own thought, can be changed through its exercise of
a knowledge that is foreign to it.[41]

Philosophy would thus be an "exercise" or "work" expended on a
knowledge foreign to it. About the non-philosophical things people
accept as true (or reject as false), philosophy would not issue a meta-
judgment "legitimating what is already known"; but by reference to
such knowledge, it would change itself. In what would its critical
attitude then consist? Foucault's answer in the last phase of his work,
is that philosophy would be that exercise or activity which, in determining the historical limits of the "thinking" foreign to it, would open the
question of new or other sorts of thinking. It would ask what other
things people might yet accept as true, what other sorts of relation to
the truth they might yet have in what they know, what they do, and
what they are. With respect to other truths, philosophy would ask: Is
it possible to think in other ways?

> [Wh]at, then, is philosophy today—I mean the activity of philosophy—
> if it is not the critical work of thought on itself? In what does it consist,
> if not, rather than legitimating what is already known, in undertaking to
> know how and to what extent it might be possible to think in other ways
> (*penser autrement*).[42]

Foucault's own historical research into "systems of thought," in any
case, would have been motivated by such a "philosophical" concern
for the truth. That is what would make his investigations into forms
of thought in their historical sites "philosophical" in a different way
from the "philosophical history" or "history of philosophy" of the last
century. Thus, in a 1978 debate with some French social historians,
Foucault declared that it was precisely this philosophical concern which
distinguished his historical project from theirs. Social historians, he
said,

> make of "society" the general horizon of their analysis and the element
> in relation to which they must locate one or another particular object
> ("society, economy, civilization"). My general theme is not society, it is

true/false discourse: I mean the correlative formation of domains, of objects and of the verifiable and falsifiable discourses that are connected to them; and it is not just this formation that interests me, but the effects of reality that are linked to it.[43]

The point of studying the historical formation of "true/false discourse" would be somewhat different from the point of studying everything in relation to "society." It would involve complications or "entanglements" of a sort which the history of society could more easily evade. Both kinds of history would involve problems of method, or of the constitution of source material, and the types of acceptable inference that can be made from it. But the "philosophical" or "critical" concern for truth in Foucault's history did not reduce to such problems of methodology. Rather, it was a matter of two senses of history; it was a question of the relation of the history he wrote to the history from which he wrote, and to which he hoped to contribute by writing. For it is there that the exercise of thinking in other ways would be deployed.

A central problem for historians and philosophers of history had been explanation; how can we explain the occurrence of events in history, and, on the basis of such explanations, what predictions can we make? Foucault was interested in another problem: Why are some things rather than others studied by historians, what kinds of "events" do they study or seek to explain? Thus, what he admired in Annales social history, or in the French history of science, was the discovery of new classes of historical events, together with new kinds of documents and styles of inference. These historians had shown for example that a change in demography or in the way bone structure was studied at different time were important historical events. In the Introduction to *The Archeology of Knowledge* he tried to isolate some common features of these two discoveries of the new sorts of things which historians might explain.

In that book, Foucault argued that there is a sense in which the question of "objects of discourse" is prior to the question of methods of explanation and prediction. In making this case, he considered himself to have discovered yet another class of events: those complex occurrences though which anonymous bodies of discourse acquire the characteristic objects for which there can be truths and falsehoods. The study of events of this kind—the "events in thought"—would involve a particular sort of critical question or questioning. It would ask: What are the events that change what we *can* explain, and the things for which we seek explanation? And the point of asking such questions would not be to make predictions, but to raise the issue of whether we need to restrict ourselves, or our ways of finding the truth, to such objects, or whether we might discover yet other new ones. The critical aim of the study of the "events in thought" would thus be to "free" our historical sense for other possibilities.

Foucault declared that what irritated people the most about his work were not so much its findings or its methods, but this critical entanglement of his "philosophy" with the events he examined. What was disturbing was his attempt "to do the history of the 'objectivization' of those elements which historians take as objectively given; . . . an entanglement (*embrouille*), in short, which it is not easy to get out of."[44]

But for Foucault, this "entanglement" with truth or objectivity was not just an epistemological matter or a question of what we can know. It was also a political entanglement, or a matter of what we can do. For Foucault had arrived at the view he expressed in a discussion about Nietzsche, that "[t]he political question, to sum up, is not error, illusion, alienated consciousness or ideology; it is truth itself."[45] This remark was directed against certain assumptions of the philosophy of *Ideologiekritik*. In exposing the "misrecognition" or "misunderstanding" people would have of their true place or role in history or society, this kind of critical philosophy, this "Interest of Reason," had supposed itself to be in possession of a "true" view of people's essential nature or social being, one that would stand outside of all "power relations." Foucault argued that it is not the case that where power is exercised, our true nature is alienated, and nothing true can be said about us. Our critical question should rather be: Why are there some sorts of truths about ourselves and not others at a time and place? And what are the costs and consequences to ourselves and our society that there exist these sorts and not others?

Thus, in his discussion with the social historians, Foucault asked: "Is not the most general political problem that of truth? How to link to one another a way of dividing up the true and the false and a manner of governing oneself and others?"[46] Since our "entanglement" with such "political" interconnection between truth and government is a matter of history, Foucault then advanced as the point of a critical examination "to discover a completely other divide through another way of governing oneself, and to govern oneself in a completely other way starting from another divide." This is what he then called the question of "political spirituality."

With this problem of "spirituality," Foucault became entangled with a third kind of truth: the sort that is involved when one is enjoined to live a "true life." It is the problem of how we can truly and freely make ourselves into certain kinds of beings; it is the problem of who we can be.

In short, the irritating entanglement of Foucault's research would consist in raising a particular "philosophical" question about the truths of which we are capable in knowledge, in politics, and in poetics. Thus, he confronted a problem for contemporary philosophy: Does there exist a distinct sort of "concern for truth" that would separate philosophy from such concerns in domains "foreign to it," in science, government and the arts? Or must we "naturalize," "politicize" or "aestheticize" philosophy, reducing its concern to one of those others? Contemporary philosophy may be said to have courted all three dangers. Some people tried to identify the critical attitude of philosophy with that of positive knowledge, and so turn it into a science; others sought to insert the critical questioning of philosophy within the assurances of a particular doctrine of society and politics, and so turn it into political theory; still others, objecting to the positivism of the first group, and the rationalism of the second, tried instead to collapse its distinctive concerns into considerations of style, writing or "poetic thinking." In each case philosophical thinking would forfeit its specificity with respect to science, political theory, or literature.

Against such reductive tendencies, Foucault sought to preserve the critical distance of philosophical thought with respect to what can be true in the thinking of science, politics, or art. That distance would not allow philosophy to dictate how truths should be pursued in these other areas. It would lie in the history of the formation of the thinking that delimits what can be true in them. By investigating that history, philosophy might ask what else can be known, can be done, or can be lived, in our historically bound activities of thought. Thus the means for Foucault's exercise or activity of "thinking in other ways" would be those of a history of particular "systems of thought." And, conversely, what he wanted to introduce into contemporary social history was precisely the existence of those "events in thought," which, by introducing new possibilities, called for the activity of such critical or philosophical intelligence.

"What is the cost to philosophy of a history of thought? What is the effect, within history, of thought and the events that belong to it?"[47] With such questions Foucault sought to formulate again the ancient problem of the very nature of philosophy. In his last lectures on *parrhesia*, he was onto a new way of charaterizing its concern for truth and of defining its characteristic *passion*.

For Foucault, "the truth" was thus not a single thing, everywhere the same. "I believe too much in the truth not to suppose that there are different truths and different ways of saying it."[48] The lectures on *parrhesia* would elaborate this distinction between different sorts of truth and different ways of saying it. Thus he introduced a grand distinction between two kinds of basic questions philosophers had raised concerning the truth. There had been a long prestigious tradition of what he called the "analytics of truth." It had been concerned with how we arrive at truths, and evaluate them. Thus Foucault himself had asked through what sorts of reasoning it is determined which things may be true or false, or about which historically constituted "objects" there can be truths, or at least "warranted assertions."

But there had also existed another type of philosophical reflection on the truth, less preeminent than the first: what Foucault called the problem of "the critical attitude to the truth." Here the question was not so much *what* is true as what it means to ourselves and the societies in which we find ourselves to *say* what is true—the risks, the consequences, in a word, the "costs" of doing do. It was this tradition that Foucault hoped to isolate and analyze: the one which asked "What does it cost for reason to tell the truth?" Such, in particular, was the problem raised in antiquity by the activities of *parrhesia*, of which Foucault isolates this general definition: *parrhesia* was the "speech-activity" in which a speaker would express his own relation to the truth at the risk even of his own life, because he held that it was a duty to do so in order to help or improve others, as well as himself.

Since at least Descartes, the prestige or primacy of the philosophy of the "analytics of truth" had served to downplay or marginalize the philosophy of the "critical attitude." We may read the *Meditations* as an attempt to sever the ancient link between the two, with the scalpel of methodological doubt. The central philosophical question would become how to square the activities of the practical subject with those of the prior theoretical one. In Antiquity, by contrast, the relation between the two would be the other way around. "In Greco-Roman culture, knowledge of oneself appeared as a consequence of taking care of yourself. In modern culture, knowledge of oneself constitutes the fundamental principle."[49]

In maintaining his critical distance from "legitimating what is already known," Foucault would rediscover something of the ancient attitude. This, in turn, helped determine what he focused on in ancient philosophy.

One effect of the Cartesian assertion of the primacy of "method" would lie in the manner in which the history of philosophy would be conceived. In the way "antiquity" came to be distinguished from "modernity," the story that leads from the great philosophers of Athens to those of Rome and Christianity would be that of decline, with little importance. For, in that centuries-long tradition in philosophical thought, the critical question of saying the truth began to separate itself from the great metaphysical doctrines as to the nature of the truth. As Foucault remarks: "Finally it came down to this: in the first century, people said: philosophy doesn't have to concern itself with truth in general but with useful truths: politics, and above all, morality."[50]

If, however, one turns one's attention away from the "analytics of truth" to the problem of its "critical attitude," then the path that leads from Athens to Rome appears not as a loss and decline into insignificance, but rather as a development in the attempt to interconnect knowledge, politics, and individual conduct, which had in fact been central to the great Athenian philosophers from Socrates to Aristotle. It is this development, marginalized in our modern conception of the history of philosophy, which Foucault tried to get at in his last lectures on *parrhesia*.

The problem of the costs and consequences of speaking the truth had been raised in many different contexts and frameworks. Sages, prophets, confessors, preachers, anarchists, psychiatrists, were all concerned with this question within practices that framed the way it was formulated. In taking up the problem, "philosophers" had to define it in contrast to these others, these "false pretenders" to the activity of speaking the truth. Thus philosophy would be part of a history of "truth-speaking practices," their emergence, ramifications, and their relations with one another.

Foucault proposed a "grid" to analyze this history that would address to it the following questions. How, in such practices, was it established *who* is entitled to speak the truth (and to whom), and under what conditions, ethical, political, or "erotic"? About what sorts of things could one thus say the truth: divine, human, natural, or whatever? What sorts of risks and consequences for oneself and society are attached to saying the truth? What sort of relation does the activity have to politics or government? Thus he would study the history of "parrhesiac thinking."

The focus of this history would then be on the "events" that opened new possibilities in such activities. Foucault's question would not simply be the social historian's question of the various roles of parrhesiac figures, and the type of "authority" they were credited with. He also wanted to examine those moments when the very assumptions that defined and delimited these practices came to be "problematized": How did people start to "take care of themselves," when the practices that provided for the who and the how of speaking the truth lost the hold of self-evidence over them?

It was with this question in mind that Foucault proposed to turn back to Socrates. Socrates was a great "parrhesiac," and was regarded as such in the long history that led to Rome. In Socrates' famous quarrels with Sophists, tragedians, politicians, indeed with anyone willing to speak of the truth with him in the Agora, we find a "problematization" of what it is to speak truly in relation to rhetoric, politics, wisdom, or poetry. With Socrates—the Socrates of the early Platonic dialogues— we find the emergence or invention of a new "parrhesiac" game with its rules, roles, and distinctive "costs." This game introduced a new way of formulating and responding to the Delphic injunction "Know yourself." It came to be called "philosophy."

What was new or distinctive about this new philosophical game? Foucault's answer is simple. Socrates introduced into the history of *parrhesia* the activity of "giving an account for oneself," of providing a *logos* for one's *bios*. Such an "account" or *logos* was, of course, not yet a Christian confession, a Cartesian meditation, or a modern psychotherapy. It did not consist in recounting the story of one's exploits in terms of the mythology of the city, and its noble genealogies; noble birth would not be essential for it. Instead it involved two principles. There was a principle of ignorance, or of the inability to account for oneself on one's own. The Socratic game thus required a master or teacher. The second principle concerned how to recognize this master. Recognition should not be based on fees or reputation, but on what Plato in the *Laches* called the "touchstone": the master is the one supposed to know how to account for himself, the one who lives his life in accordance or harmony with his *logos*, the one who thus lives "truly."

Unlike the rhetoritician or Sophist, the philosophical master thus had to himself believe what he taught. Unlike the prophet, he had to speak in his own name, and not about the future that will come, but about the concrete present in which he finds himself. Unlike the sage, whose esoteric pronouncements on what there is involves an endless interpretation, he had to concern himself with the concrete "ignorance" in which each person finds himself.

"The unexamined life is not worth living," Socrates declared. But what is it to "examine" a life, and what are its "costs"? These were questions people would ask themselves for a long time. Plato would provide one answer, Aristotle another, but the question would remain unsettled; it would undergo many reformulations and transformations. In some sense Foucault's own attempt to "think in other ways" would be an instance of it: the unexamined life would be the one where one is content to think the same. "The critical function of philosophy up to a certain point emerges right from the Socratic imperative."[51]

In reconstituting the parrhesiac figure of Socrates as a sort of nodal point in the schools and traditions of ancient thought, it was this *question* of philosophy, and of its "critical attitude" that Foucault wanted to keep alive. He wanted to study how for centuries it would remain controversial just what sort of relation Socratic "truth-saying" should have with knowledge, with the city and its government, and with the "poetry" of creating a noble existence. And it is just in this respect that the ancient problem of Socratic *parrhesia* would discover its lineages with Foucault's own problem of the "entanglement" of his critical activity in "knowledge foreign to it": in science, in politics, and in living.

Foucault spoke of "fishing around" in ancient thought, looking again for what seems worth keeping or reviving, and what abandoning or historicizing. He thought that this question should today be raised in a different way from the great Romantic and post-Kantian philosophical preoccupation with Antiquity, with its problems of ancient "community" and modern "morality." At one point he put the matter in terms of the liberation movements with which his own critical philosophy had been involved:

> Well, I wonder if our problem nowadays is not, in a way, similar to this [ancient] one, since most of us no longer believe that ethics is founded in religion, nor do we want a legal system to intervene in our moral, personal, private life. Recent liberation movements suffer from the fact that they cannot find any principle on which to base the elaboration of a new ethics. They need an ethics, but they cannot find any other ethics than an ethics founded on so-called scientific knowledge of what the self is, what desire is, what the unconscious is, and so on. I am struck by this similarity of problems.[52]

Part of the motivation of Foucault's last lectures on *parrhesia* would reside in this problem of critical discourse in such a situation, where the question of a "true" manner of living would be raised again. They would supply something of a "genealogy" of his own philosophy, regarded as a species of free critical speech. Can we today invent a free discourse that would take up again the question of the art of living, through an activity of thought which would not base its way of speaking truly on any given positive knowledge about ourselves or our world, or on any theory of government presumed to be final and sufficient, a critical philosophy that in questioning such knowledge and such theory, would open new possibilities in what we might become?

Plato had introduced Socratic free speech into three great areas that would become traditional for philosophy: knowledge, politics, poetry. Thus he advanced his anti-Sophistic doctrine of Forms, his new foundation for the City, and his arguments for the banishment of the poets from it. It is the same areas with which Foucault would continue to be preoccupied in the critical entanglements of his own practice of thought. Starting from this initial Platonic response to the question of philosophy, we may thus gather together some of the fragments of Foucault's "fishing around" in ancient thought, finding thereby his own attitude to each domain of philosophical investigation.

A. Knowledge

Plato inserted the Socratic activity of providing an account for one's living within the framework of a general theory of knowledge or *episteme*, modeled in part on geometry, and resulting in the postulation of Forms. To know was for the soul to recall such Forms or Ideas which it had forgotten in a pre-existence; and to accomplish this it had to "reorient" itself, rediscovering its true relation to itself. Thus, Plato helped initiate a "contemplative" tradition in philosophy, where an ascesis is required for the soul to know anything.

Descartes would break with this part of the Platonic inheritance. "Certainty" would replace "wisdom" in the meditational monologue Descartes proposed for any thinking being. Through a "method," anyone could learn to separate his true from his false ideas. The "critical attitude" would consist, or at least, start in this exercise in methodological doubt. Ancient *parrhesia* had not found this problem important; it was rather concerned with the courage of saying the truth in the face of political or moral dangers.

Foucault's "critical attitude" would be of another sort. It would arise from a generalized contemporary crisis in the Cartesian or methodological conception of the critical relation to knowledge. Foucault wanted to replace the Cartesian search for a method leading to the subjective attitude of certainty with the question of the historical constitution of "objects of knowledge." What secures the objects of knowledge would be an anonymous regularity in thinking not rooted in a subject's—even a transcendental subject's—relation to himself. "Objectivity" in knowledge would be based in such regularities,and would not be defined by a basic or founding "subjectivity," even if some rules concerned the sort of subjects who may make objective assertions.

Foucault's critical attitude would thus contrast with the "positivism" which, while it had also sought to eliminate "psychologism," had preserved the search for a single invariant method of inference, or relation to experience, which would be found in all knowledge, and perhaps even in all "meaningful" discourse. Foucault took up the work of the new historians of science who disputed the assumption of the methodological unity of knowledge, and who held that it was not the possession of an "algorithm of appraisal," but a history, that constituted objectivity in science. Foucault said knowledge was "dispersed" or disunified; and that a logic of inference (deductive or inductive) was never enough to account for the thinking that made it objective.

He then focused not on "noble" sciences such as physics or mathematics, but on much less formalized sorts of knowledge concerning madness, illness, crime and sex. In relation to such objects at least, the critical aim of studying the thinking that advanced them would be of a new sceptical sort. Unlike Cartesian scepticism, it would not be a question of arriving at certainty, and would not be concerned with Knowledge in general, but with specific kinds of it, and the discourses related to it. For in such cases, what can be known is tied to what can be done, and such knowledge-power is directed to the conception of particular forms of experience people have of themselves. Foucault's scepticism was directed to the certainty or assurance that this was the only way to conceptualize these forms of experience, the only way to obtain truths about them. This would become a first aspect of Foucault's critical philosophical activity: its specific scepticism concerning the thinking which makes certain kinds of basic experience susceptible to knowledge. This pluralizing scepticism would then confront a second problem: that of the kinds of power which such "positivities" in knowledge suppose and help to establish. As such, it would become a "political" matter; it would discover a new sort of political *parrhesia*.

B. Politics

Another area into which Plato inserted Socratic *parrhesia* was politics. He advanced the principle, enshrined in the soul/city analogy, that those who know how to "account for themselves," and therefore how to wisely master or govern themselves, should be the ones to rule those who cannot. Thus, he introduced a change in the framework of the debate surrounding *parrhesia,* over the risks of speaking freely in assemblies or in giving advice to a king.

This change is shown in Book IX of the *Republic,* where Plato objects to democracy. Others had already argued that since the *demos* includes the worst, what is best for the *demos* cannot be best for the *polis.* Thus Isocrates had held that the courageous orator is in fact the one who opposes the *demos.* Plato introduced another line of thought and argument: the real danger of democracy would not be that it leads to bad decisions or to corrupt or ignorant rulers, but that it induces a democratic "way of life," a democratic *ethos.* The danger of this way of living is that it would ruin the unity or common *logos* of the city, the danger that there would be as many constitutions as there are citizens. Thus, Plato made *parrhesia* not simply a problem of oratory, but a problem of the soul's relation to itself. He connected the freedom to say what one wills *(parrhesia)* to the irresponsible freedom to do as one pleases, without regard for "the true life." That is why the analogy between the city and the soul would govern his account of political constitutions. That account would involve the problem of "political spirituality," or the inherent link between the truth one speaks and who one is.

This problem of "political spirituality" would have a long history. Ancient "civic culture" would erode and Christianity would pose the problem in other terms, as in what Paul Veyne has called "the democracy of shame."[53] In particular, Foucault held that with the figure of the "politician" who manages the "policies" of a modern state, there would be a break or crisis in the ancient view of political virtue. The "accountability" of running a state would no longer be thought to essentially depend on the capacity of the politician to give an "account" for his life, or on the variants of the practice developed in Rome.

In these altered historical conditions, critical philosophical activity in politics would assume another role, or define for itself another kind of philosophical "responsibility." It would seek to determine and to maintain limits on the "excesses" of the political management of the state. It is in this context that the terms "critique" or "critical theory" would enter the lexicon of philosophy's conception of its political task.

Since Kant the role of philosophy is to prevent reason from going beyond the limits of experience. But at the same moment—that is since the development of the modern state and the political management of society—the role of philosophy is also to keep watch over the excessive powers of political rationality. Which is a rather high expectation.[54]

Foucault wrote from a sense of crisis in the high expectations placed in post-Kantian political critique; his analysis of the "anthropological slumbers" in this tradition was an early diagnosis of it. The difficulty would lie in the attempt to insert political philosophical critique into a grand history of the West, whose *telos* would be given by the social being of Man. In the post-Kantian tradition, one had imagined that the critical link between freedom and truth, and so "spirituality," resided in some "utopian" place, prior to the exercise of power and its ideologies, which one would then call upon History to realize. Foucault took the crisis in this grand philosophical project to be a crisis in the role of the "intellectual," the figure who had emerged with the Dreyfus affair, and who had assumed the philosophical task Kant had set for the *Aufklärer*. His questioning of the assumptions of *Ideologiekritik* was an attempt to sharpen our sense of this problematization. His distinction between specific and universal intellectuals was one response to it.

Foucault found in Nietzsche a philosopher who had questioned "the two great problems of nineteenth century philosophy, passed on by Fichte and Hegel (the reciprocal basis of truth and freedom, and the possibility of absolute knowledge)."[55] Nietzsche thus introduced a type of critical thought that did not look in Man or Society for a utopian "spirituality" outside of power. He was a "philosopher of power, a philosopher who managed to think of power without having to enclose himself within a political theory to do so."[56]

In taking up this theme, Foucault would say we no longer need to think in terms of the progress or the decline of a single great Truth or Rationality in general.

It may not be wise to take as a whole the rationalization of society or of culture, but to analyze such a process in several fields, each with reference to a fundamental experience: madness, illness, death, crime, sexuality, and so forth.[57]

In regard to such "specific rationalities," critical thought, in the absence of a grand theory, would then raise a particular kind of question. It would emerge in the new social movements or struggles. Foucault thought that such struggles did not arise in, and were not tied to, any single type of government; that they did not have the "high expectation" of a final liberation from all power; that there were directed to the kinds of "individuality" history makes possible; and that they thus raise a critical question as to who we are and may be. In this they would discover in a new way the Nietzschean critique of power without the assurance of political theory. For through them there would arise "a plurality of questions posed to politics rather than a reinscription of the act of questioning within the framework of a political doctrine."[58]

Thus a new type of political *parrhesia* would become possible. It would hold that no theory or no effective practice of government should be allowed to arrogate for itself the right to know and to regulate a single general truth as to how best to live, and the social arrangements in which it is possible. Rather one would be attentive to those moments when, within a given situation of power, people start to question their social arrangements and their participation in maintaining them, without possessing a theory to tell them in advance what to do.

> Nothing is more inconsistent than a political regime that is indifferent to the truth; but nothing is more dangerous than a political system that claims to prescribe the truth. The function of "free speech" doesn't have to take legal form, just as it would be vain to believe that it resides by right in spontaneous exchanges of communication. The task of speaking the truth is an infinite labor: to respect it in its complexity is an obligation that no power can afford to shortchange, unless it would impose the silence of slavery.[59]

C. Poetry

In his last research, Foucault tried to isolate what, following Plutarch, he called the "etho-poetic" tradition in philosophy, in which *poesis*, or the work of artistic creation, would serve as a *model* for living well, as well as a *technique* in the accomplishment of this fundamental task of ancient "virtue." How did Socratic free speech figure in the attempt to make of one's *ethos* a beautiful work that posterity might admire? In the lectures on *parrhesia*, Foucault drew a contrast between two general strategies that would assume their most stark form in the challenge of Cynicism to Platonism. He distinguished a "psycho-metaphysical" from a "bio-aesthetic" use of Socratic *parrhesia*. Each use offered a particular way of responding to the advice of the Delphic Oracle to know yourself, and thus to a particular image of the "true life," associated in Plato, respectively, with the *Alcibiades* and the *Laches*. Each would involve a different passion in one's relation to the truths one might say of oneself, a different sort of "cost."

The first use of the "Socratic method" was turned towards the contemplation of the soul in the great metaphysical divide between Appearance and Reality. Thus, there would be the image of the soul escaping the prison of the body in order to see again the Forms it had forgotten. The second was concerned not so much with the soul as with life, and not so much with contemplation as with a sort of practical testing or experimentation to determine whether one's life was in accord or harmony with the truths one was capable of saying about it. Thus, there would be the image of a life imprisoned in the unnecessary servitude of habitual or inherited ways of living, and the attempt to "stylize" both body and soul in a departure that would expose such servitude. The second or bio-aesthetic sort of "concern for truth," or *parrhesia*, was thus preoccupied not with "another world," but with another manner of living. As such it was elaborated by the Cynics and opposed to the "psycho-metaphysical" or "contemplative" practices.

From Cynicism there remains little by way of ethical doctrine or metaphysics. Rather there are stories that recount a way of life, and the critical attitude it embodied, the point of which is to show that a person is at bottom nothing else than the relation to the truth which gives his life its shape and form. The principle of Cynicism was that the "true life" was not the otherworldly contemplative life, but the scandalous one, opposed to the inveterate hypocrisies of custom.

As such the cynical idea was to have a long if unnoticed history. It would be found in the Christian mendicants and heretics who contradicted public norms of living. The early Christians would adapt cynical *parrhesia* to the new practice of preaching, applying it not simply to a privileged minority, but to everyone. The same tradition would also be found in nineteenth-century anarchism, where scandalous or asocial lifestyles where thought to be prophetic of a new age and so critical of the present one. In the arts, "cynical" themes would appear in the theatre of the eighteenth century, and would later recur in "modern art," where the work of the artist would be thought part of his life, or of his "avant-garde" identity. Contemporary "counter-cultural" or "alternative" activities would then reactivate the theme in yet other ways.

In particular, Foucault hoped to rediscover this tradition in the modern "experience of poetry," shown in the link between Baudelaire and *dandysme*. Indeed, one may say that along these lines, he hoped to reread his earlier discussion, in concert with Maurice Blanchot, of the replacement of the Romantic idea of "genius" with the more anonymous "author" of *l'absence d'oeuvre*. For here there would be an experience of oneself in the activity of writing that would not seek to base itself on any pregiven "theory of the subject," but would rather start from the specific moments of critical "transcendence" in historically given modes or styles of existence.

Of neither Plato nor Aristotle could it be said that they cultivated the use of writing in this way as a "practice of the self"; the practice of *écriture* was not important for their notion of how to live truly. Foucault disputes the view that a distinction between writing and speaking truly was a central one for them. He argues that the *hypomnemata* to which Plato refers in the *Phaedrus* were in fact notebooks or memoranda in which one jotted down advice and sayings in order to better administer one's life. Plato's question was whether or not they were suited for the task of true self-government, and it was only in this precise form that they figured in the debates about the techniques of writing within a culture of memory.

It is only starting around the first century A.D., according to Foucault, that writing as a "practice of the self" would start to have wide currency in philosophy; it is to be found in Seneca, Epectetus, and Marcus Aurelius. Later, Christianity would invent new forms such as keeping a diary or journal in one's "spiritual exercises." Writing things down would thus start to become an important instrument in the attempts to freely form a "true life." It would become an integral part of

Montaigne's "scepticism." Foucault came to see his own activity of writing as part of this tradition, or as "autobiographical" in this sense. To the sceptical and political activity of his critical *parrhesia* would thus belong a "poetic" one, concerned with the formation of his own "subjectivity." In his attempts to "think in other ways," he would adopt the rather cynical principle that says "to live well is to kill psychology."

Foucault did not speak of an end of philosophy or of "metaphysics." He saw such talk as part of a hermeneutic enterprise which pictured the tradition as successive interpretations of original sources, whose forgotten or hidden truth it would try to expose.

> Nothing is more foreign to me than the idea that philosophy strayed at a certain moment of time, and that it has forgotten something and that somewhere in its history there exists a principle, a basis that must be rediscovered.[60]

The question of truth in the history of philosophy should be raised in another way. One would not try to historicize philosophy by inserting its events into a single great interpretative scheme one would then have to surpass or overcome. Rather one would try to "eventalize" the history of philosophy by finding again the external events that caused it to rethink itself and to ask what else it is possible to think. It was this sort of critical exercise, this sort of "perilous act" that Foucault wanted to rediscover and to reinvent in philosophy.

Plato had introduced Socratic *parrhesia* into knowledge, politics and poetry. Many centuries later, Foucault would diagnose a crisis in the relation of philosophy to each area. A new kind of *parrhesia*, a new type of critical discourse would then become possible: sceptical about the institutions of informal knowledge, problematizing the strategies of government, and counter-psychological in the free poetry of living. And so Foucault would be confronted with a fourth and, since Plato, an equally traditional question in philosophy—What is the *eros* of thinking; what is the *passion* of critical thought?

D. Eros

In his first lecture-course at the Collège de France, Foucault declared that he wanted to set aside as vague and imprecise such traditional

notions of the passion for truth as the "need for mastery and appropria-
tion through knowledge," or "distress before the unknown," or the
"spirit of the period." Even psychoanalysis had not yet provided a
useful idea.

In their place, Foucault drew a contrast between an Aristotelian
conception of the "pleasure in theoretical contemplation" supposed to
be natural to Man, and a Nietzschean conception of the "will to
knowledge." This "will" would be neither contemplative nor natural,
nor everywhere the same. Rather, knowledge would be seen as an
"invention," and as an "event, or at the very least, a series of events."
It would be fundamentally "interested," and its "interest" would involve a basic and paradoxical "falsification" of experience, that would
allow people to say truths of some things but not of others. It was,
then, such features of the "will to knowledge" that Foucault hoped
to develop in the course of his concrete historical studies of various
"discursive practices."[61]

Six years later, after much hesitation, Foucault decided to entitle the
first and introductory volume of his *History of Sexuality* "*La volonté
de savoir*" (the will to knowledge). What then would this will have to
do with eros and with its history?

Antiquity had made of Eros a central topic for the activity of philosophy. Eros would have a part in each of the areas in which Socratic
parrhesia was exercised; and one could thus speak of the eros of the
one who knows, who masters himself and others, and who affirms the
beauty of his noble virile freedom. It was in this erotico-pedagogical
context that Foucault placed the Platonic turn to contemplation. In his
analysis of "true love" in the *Phaedrus* and the *Symposium*, Foucault
tried to trace the arguments through which the aesthetic problem of
pederastic courtship, with its difficulties of status and passivity, would
be replaced by the metaphysical problem of the inherent link between
eros and an otherworldly existence. Throughout antiquity, he says,
there was not much *amour fou*; one must wait for Ovid for

> the moment when you have the possibility and the opening of an experi-
> ence in which the individual completely loses his head in some way, no
> longer knows who he is, is unaware of his identity, and lives his lover's
> experiences as a perpetual forgetting of self. Now that's a later experience
> that in no way corresponds to that of Plato and Aristotle.[62]

There would be many avenues through which eros would enter contemporary philosophy. Existentialism and phenomenology would refer to it in their attempts to oppose the "lived body" to the disembodied Cartesian thinking subject. Following Romanticism, it would be thought part of what it is to be a "genius" or "poet." The liberation movements would make it important for "critical theory." With the *erotisme* of Georges Bataille, it would play a part in the modern questioning of the subject; it would constitute a philosophical "event" in that it helped to introduce the question of the "limits of experience" through which the modern philosophical privilege of the subject was challenged. Thus, in the sixties, Foucault would refer to "modern sexuality from Sade to Freud": what would characterize it was not to have liberated the true nature of sex, but rather to have "denatured" it, making it a limit of experience.

> We have not in the least liberated sexuality, though we have, to be exact, carried it to its limits: the limits of consciousness, because it ultimately dictates the only possible reading of our unconscious; the limit of law, because it seems the sole substance of universal taboos; the limit of language, since it traces the line of foam showing just how far speech may advance upon the sands of silence. Thus, it is not through sexuality that we communicate with the orderly and pleasingly profane world of animals; rather, sexuality is a fissure—not one which surrounds us as the basis of our isolation or individuality, but one which marks the limit with us and designates as limit.[63]

In rethinking this idea of limits and their "transgression," Foucault came, in his last work, to see eros rather in relation to a parrhesiac situation, not so unlike the one with which Socrates had confronted the young Plato. In rejecting the great modern injunction to be true or faithful to our desire, we would want, as with Socrates, a critical activity of thought, which would not find its basis in religion, government, or science, in ecclesiastic, political or positivistic authority. We would require a kind of philosophical activity to maintain a sceptical distance with respect to the positive knowledge of sexuality offered by doctors, social workers, statisticians, psychiatrists or gurus. We would need a philosophical activity that would allow us to maintain a critical distance from the constitution of sexuality in strategies of government.

And finally we would want a philosophy that could use such sceptical and political distance in freely creating new ways of living.

In this manner we might again become uncertain and curious as to how to tell the truth about our eros, and the eros of doing so. And so we might give a more precise sense of the "wonderment" or "bewilderment" through which philosophy had sought to describe the passion to know, or the "will to knowledge." We might define a kind of critical "curiosity,"

> the only kind of curiosity worth practicing with a little obstinacy: not the one which seeks to assimilate itself with what is proper to know, but the one which allows one to disengage oneself from oneself (se déprendre de soi-même). What would the relentlessness of knowledge (l'acharnement du savoir) be worth it were to secure only the acquisition of knowledge and not, in a certain manner and as much as it can, the straying (égarement) of the one who knows?[64]

The eros of Foucault's philosophy, its peculiar "will to truth," would reside in this curious, experimental, critical passion to freely disengage oneself from oneself, discovering again what is possible to know, to do, or to be. Thus, in the bonds of those brought together in the practice of freedom would lie a characteristic "concern for truth," a *parrhesia*, of which it may be said that:

(1) It would not consist in an expertise in the solution to our problems, but would turn its "curiosity" to the unnoticed dangers in the precise techniques we employ to conceive and resolve our problems, to those questionable and questioning areas of experience for which we do not already have accepted or acceptable "procedures of solution."

(2) It would not consist in an esoteric wisdom to which one must convert as to a school or sect, but would start its "curiosity" rather from an experience of "deconversion," from a loss of assurance or certainty as to who we are and may be, opening up spaces in which no one is as yet the master.

(3) It would not consist in a nostalgia for what has been, or in a prophesy or prediction as to what must come, but would direct its "curiosity" to those problematizing events that emerge in the midst of our history, initiating new and unforeseen possibilities.

(4)   It would not consist in the contemplation of a Reason from
which to derive rules and norms applicable to all, and from
which none could dissent, but would deploy its "curiosity" in
those new areas of experience that question the "reason" of
the rules or norms we have adopted, and so might require us
to invent other ones.

In the restless, unfinished ruminations and studies, in the many
interviews and lectures, as in the "books of history" of Foucault's last
years, it was this passion, this philosophical "curiosity" concerning the
truth, which Foucault sought to define and to put into practice. Thus
would his own singular eros, and his own singular way of doing
philosophy, come together for a last time.

The Question of Ethics

Why have I reviewed this work that goes back over a half-century, its original contexts now receding from us to become the topic of biographies and histories? It is not to promote a new orthodoxy, a new Master to tell us what to do. On the contrary, I wanted to isolate in it something that might yet engage our thought today: "the question of ethics."

There may be many things to recommend moral theory; one is not to have raised this question. The piety of moral theory is to try to say what is good for each and all of us, and where and how to find it. Our experience matters for such theory only to the degree that it conforms, or fails to conform, to such theoretical goods or obligations. The question of who we are—historically, libidinally or "aesthetically"— is a secondary one. A different sort of philosophy is to be found in Lacan and Foucault.

I have tried to show that the question of ethics is what is most "difficult" in the work of Lacan and Foucault: the least resolved, the most open. Yet, at the same time, it is the most intimate or "subjective," the most closely linked to the singularities of their style or the peculiarities of their writing; it is the part that leads most directly to the question of "truth" and so to the passion of their thought. A point of intersection or contact is to be found in a sense of impasse in the promise of psychoanalysis in France, which came to a head around 1975–6.

In the way of thinking each elaborates, the question of ethics arises with the discovery of something that would be irreducible to the "constitution of the subject" in the order of language, or in historical systems of thought, and so to the symbolic or discursive "idealism" that says we are only what a culture makes us be. In Foucault there would be those moments of "transcendence" in the midst of our concrete histories; in Lacan, the *jouissance en plus*, that "necessity" a civilization or "social bond" can never elude. Thus, there is Lacan's "realism" of what must always be left out in our self-idealization, and

Foucault's "pragmatism" concerning what is yet free in our historical determinations.

It is to these realistic or pragmatic junctures that they bring the question of subjectivity—that is where they raise the question of who we are, of our freedom with respect to who or what we are said to be, and the bonds of which we are thus capable. And so they direct the passion of their thought to an analysis of what in our experience exceeds our identification with our ways of life, opening them to questioning and transformation, without the assurance of an ideal "Platonic Republic."

In this unsettling of our identities would lie the problem of a "new erotics": of a new type of bond not based on the exigencies of the super-ego; or a new type of community not based on what we already know of ourselves and the ways we have come to govern ourselves. In the "beauty" of our tragic libidos or historical fatalities, would thus lie an attempt to rethink the ancient question of *ethos*: how to be "at home" in a world where our identity is not given, our being-together in question, our destiny contingent or uncertain: the world of the violence of our own self-constitution. Such would be a question that we still today ignore only at the cost of a murderous brutality.

For it may be argued that the thirst for an unproblematic or "fundamental" identity, in those situations that raise the question of identity, has been a source of the most horrendous terror of which we have shown ourselves capable. Its impulses are shown in the fear that someone is taking this identity from us, introducing an "other" passion or subjectivity in which it would be lost; or in the supposition that someone knows about it, knows how to extirpate or rid what prevents us from having it. The question of a "new erotics" is the question of how to live without such a supposition of identity, or where it is made the object of analysis. And, conversely, to analyze this root of our "archaisms" or "fundamentalisms" is to rethink the question of subjectivity, and of our bonds with one another.

To rethink subjectivity in this way is thus not to postulate what we must be, but to introduce another type of thinking. There exists no Theory in the traditional sense for what in our "desire" exceeds our "good," or for what is "intolerable" in our historically determined being. That is why Lacan wanted to extract ethics from *Bien-dire*, and

Foucault, critical intelligence from the idealistic formation of a political will.

And so they diagnose a crisis in our ethical thought of a particular kind, a crisis not so much in the rational grounds for asserting our ideals or the method of their application to cases, as in what they mean to us and our experience of ourselves: their costs, their consequences, their limits. Thus they promote a "suspiciousness" concerning the demands that give rise to moral theory, and the sense of the degree to which such theory satisfies, or can satisfy, these demands. It is just this "Nietzschean" sort of suspicion which Bernard Williams now tells us that the "received pieties" of contemporary moral theory has forfeited; it has been left—unfortunately, Williams thinks—to the "historical and literary studies" influenced by the likes of Foucault and Lacan.[1]

In moral philosophy there has been "applied ethics" in what Williams sees as the "unhelpful form" of deriving abstract principles from cases and casting them in terms of a general theory or method of reasoning. There have been questions of equity in law and justice, and the "spheres" to which they apply. Over what, it has been asked, should the writ of moral theory range? There have been arguments over whether or not governments should avoid all conceptions as to "the good life." But what has not been asked is whether there can be anything new in ethics.

It is sometimes said that we today live among different ethical traditions without being able to say any longer why we should adopt them, or how to choose among them. "Pluralism" is the view that we should keep all of them at once, even if at the price of logical dissonance or "incommensurability"; "monism" is the view that we need or must have the single correct theory. But in neither case does there arise the problem of what might yet come to reshuffle and rethink our traditions. The ethical thought of Foucault and Lacan is not meant to preclude, replace or "destroy" all others, but to raise this question. The "question of ethics" is always the question of what can be new in ethics, and so involves a "suspiciousness" about received values, as has always been the case.

Thus we must not suppose that our history is restricted to what is already known about us. Our history is such that we cannot choose from past possibilities as from a catalogue (we in fact always start somewhere), and such that we cannot project ahead an ideal to resolve in advance all problems that will confront us (there in fact exists no such ideal). We are not condemned to think that only Tradition or Eternity can tell us who we are and what is worthwhile about our existence; we are not condemned to what Nietzsche called "*ressentiment.*"

Indeed we need not submit to the blackmail of "folkways" that tells us that without them we can have no identity, or the blackmail of abstract principles that tells us without *them* we can have no independent way of criticizing our folkways. The "we" of the "question of ethics" is not given through the specious "Hegelian" alternative between universal principles and particular communities, between "rationalism" and "relativism." For it is in some sense "we" ourselves that are always in question, we ourselves whose experience is always departing from our identifications. What new forms of bonds, what new sorts of rules may we yet invent for ourselves, do we yet *want* to have?

The ancient Master was the one to know how to master the excesses of experience in temperate wisdom. In dissociating itself from such wisdom, philosophy would become "academic," propounding theories modeled on a modern Science, as in the sort of Alexandrian "meta-ethics" from which Wittgenstein recoiled, attracting disciples.

But the philosophies of Foucault and Lacan would require another social form: not a school with its Master, not a University with its Experts. Lacan distrusted ecclesiastical authority, the "Church" of Psychoanalysis; Foucault rejected the Party with its presumption to subordinate all "specific" political agency. Their work belongs to a crisis in ethical thought: Can there exist an ethical "authority" or "mastery" that would be neither bureaucratic nor charismatic, neither scientific nor mediatic? Can there exist a truth that would not be that of a timeless ideal to which we must aspire, or that of a traditional role we must assume, but would rather be a condition of "the question" which confronts us with this other we might yet become? To make the "question of ethics" an unavoidable part of ethics, no longer separating who we think we are from what we think is proper to do or good to be—such would be the modern form of Mastery of the ancient Socratic principle that the unexamined life is not worth living.

One thing is for sure: we are not yet done with this problem of our identity, this difficulty with ourselves, our concrete freedom and our bonds with one another. We are not yet done with the question of what was once called our "spirituality."

On the contrary, even if academic philosophy has been somewhat disappointing in its response to it, never has the "question of ethics" been more alive or more free. We want to put behind us the secular ideologies of perfection, and what led us into the European war and its genocide. Yet it is not certain what categories we have to conceive of what would come after, of what we are becoming.

New waves of immigration and the creation of new forms of poverty and misery have again created "communities" whose identity is in question, occasioning fears and anxieties as to "who we are." Perhaps the general symptom of this crisis is the impasse that combines a resurgence of fundamentalisms with the comfortable "consensus" that all we need are the good old nineteenth-century ideals of market, law and parliamentary democracy. To analyze and to emerge from this impasse, we might again require the type of "suspicious" critical intelligence that returns us to what in our concrete experience exceeds what we agree, accept and know.

Perhaps we need a kind of thinking that is not content to leave the question of who we are to moral theorists, but would introduce it into the heart of an ethical thought whose principle is that injustice is first and without end; an ethic that substitutes for the search for values independent of our experience the questions our concrete sufferings and oppressions would introduce into our claims to rights or to justice; an ethic that introduces the question of legality where there is only the rule of law, the question of government where there is only the exercise of power, and the question of self-invention where there is only the workings of knowledge.

In this way, we might be able to raise again the questions that haunted Lacan and Foucault: What is the place of eros—of *jouissance*, of our suffering and pleasure—in the truths by which we live? What is the place of truth in the ways we have invented to live together?

Notes

Introduction

1. Jacques Lacan, *Ecrits* (Norton, 1977), p. 146.
2. Michel Foucault, *Foucault Live,* ed. Sylvère Lotringer (Semiotext(e), 1989), p. 303.
3. *Ibid.,* p. 317.
4. Gilles Deleuze, *Pourparlers* (Minuit, 1990), p. 116.
5. Foucault, *Foucault Live,* p. 303.
6. Michel Foucault, *The Foucault Reader,* ed. Paul Rabinow (Pantheon, 1984), p. 339.
7. Michel Foucault, "The Ethic of the Care for the Self as a Practice of Freedom," in *Philosophy and Social Criticism,* vols. 2–3 (Summer 1987), p. 131.
8. Michel Foucault, *Technologies of the Self,* eds. Luther H. Martin, Huck Gutman and Patrick H. Hutton (University of Massachusetts, 1988), p. 22.
9. *Ibid.*
10. Foucault, *Foucault Live,* p. 206.
11. Quoted in Didier Eribon, *Michel Foucault* (Flammarion, 1989), p. 239.
12. Foucault, *Foucault Live,* pp. 245–46.
13. Foucault, *Technologies of the Self,* p. 17.
14. Michel Foucault, "Afterword," in H. Dreyfus and P. Rabinow, *Michel Foucault: Beyond Structuralism and Hermeneutics* (Chicago, 1982), p. 216.
15. Foucault, *Foucault Live,* p. 303.
16. Quoted in Jacques Lagrange, "Versions de la psychanalyse dans le texte de Foucault," in *Psychanalyse à L'université* (April 1987), p. 279.
17. Jacques Lacan, *Télévision* (Seuil, 1974), pp. 47–48.
18. *Ibid.,* p. 49.
19. *Ibid.,* p. 65.
20. Lacan, *Ecrits,* p. 7 (translation modified).

21. Jacques Lacan, Compte rendu avec interpolations du Seminaire de L'Ethique," in *Ornicar*, vol. 28 (Primptemps, 1984), p. 13.

22. Jacques Lacan, *The Four Fundamental Concepts of Psychoanalysis* (Norton, 1981), p. 33.

23. Lacan, "Compte rendu," p. 15.

24. Jacques Lacan, "Impromtu at Vincennes," *October,* vol. 40 (Spring, 1987), p. 126.

25. Michel Foucault, P. *Language, Counter-Memory, Practice,* ed. D. Bouchard (Cornell, 1977), p. 133.

26. *Ibid.*, p. 134.

27. *Ibid.*, p. 136.

28. *Ibid.*

29. Lacan, *The Four Fundamental Concepts,* p. 12.

30. *Ibid.*, p. 28.

31. Lacan, *Télévision*, p. 36.

Part 1: Lacan

1. Jacques Lacan, *Encore* (Seuil, 1975), p. 9.

2. Jacques Lacan, *L'Ethique de la Psychanalyse* (Seuil, 1986), p. 71.

3. Jacques Lacan, "Compte rendu avec interpolations du Seminaire de L'Ethique," in *Ornicar*, vol. 28 (Primptempts, 1984), p. 8.

4. Lacan, *L'Ethique de la Psychanalyse,* p. 17.

5. Michel Foucault, *The Birth of the Clinic* (Pantheon, 1973), p. 198.

6. *Ibid.*, p. 172.

7. *Ibid.*

8. Lacan, "Compte rendu," p. 14.

9. *Ibid.*

10. See Bernard Williams, "Philosophy," in *The Legacy of Greece: A New Appraisal,* ed. M. I. Finley (Oxford, 1981), pp. 202–5.

11. Jacques Lacan, *Ecrits* (Norton, 1977), p. 49.

12. *Ibid.*

13. Lacan, "Compte rendu," p. 14.

14. Sigmund Freud, *Totem and Taboo* (Pantheon, 1946), p. 205.

15. Jacques Lacan, *Télévision* (Seuil, 1974), p. 51.

16. Quoted in Jacques-Alain Miller, "Reponse du réel," in *Aspects du Malaise dans la Civilisation* (Navarin, 1987), p. 9.

17. Lacan, *L'Ethique de la Psychanalyse*, pp. 20–21.

18. Lacan, *Télévision*, p. 51.

19. Lacan, *Encore*, p. 39.

20. Lacan, *L'Ethique de la Psychanalyse*, p. 64.

21. Lacan, *Télévision*, p. 16.

22. *Ibid.*

23. *Ibid.*, p. 6.

24. Jacques Lacan, *Scilicet*, vols. 6–7 (Seuil, 1974), p. 38.

25. Lacan, *Encore*, p. 78.

26. *Ibid.*, p. 81.

27. *Ibid.*, p. 78.

28. Lacan, *L'Ethique de la Psychanalyse*, p. 13.

29. Lacan, *Encore*, p. 78.

30. *Ibid.*, p. 58.

31. *Ibid.*, p. 80.

32. *Ibid.*, p. 76.

33. *Ibid.*

34. *Ibid.*, p. 78.

35. *Ibid.*, p. 77.

36. Jacques Lacan, "Kant avec Sade," in *Ecrits II* (Seuil, 1966), p. 125.

37. Lacan, *Télévision*, p. 48.

38. *Ibid.*

39. Lacan, *Encore*, p. 55.

40. *Ibid.*, p. 56.

41. Jeremy Bentham, *A Fragment on Government* (Oxford, 1951), p. 63.

42. Lacan, *Encore*, p. 10.

43. Jeremy Bentham, *An Introduction to the Principles of Morals and Legislation*, (Athlone, 1970), p. 7.

44. Ian Hacking, *The Taming of Chance* (Cambridge, 1990).

45. Jacques-Alain Miller, "Jeremy Bentham's Panoptic Device," *October*, vol. 41 (Summer 1987).

46. Lacan, "Compte rendu," p. 12.

47. Lacan, *Encore*, p. 55.

48. *Ibid.*, p. 57.
49. Lacan, "Compte rendu," p. 15.
50. Lacan, *L'Ethique de la Psychanalyse*, p. 105.
51. *Ibid.*, pp. 128–29.
52. *Ibid.*, p. 110.
53. *Ibid.*, p. 133.
54. Lacan, *Encore*, p. 70.
55. *Ibid.*
56. Lacan, *L'Ethique de la Psychanalyse*, p. 126.
57. *Ibid.*, pp. 126–27.
58. *Ibid.*, p. 301.
59. Lacan, *Télévision*, p. 27.
60. Lacan, *L'Ethique de la Psychanalyse*, p. 85.
61. *Ibid.*, p. 17.

Part 2: Foucault

1. Michel Foucault, *Foucault Live,* ed. Sylvère Lotringer (Semiotext(e), 1989), p. 249.
2. Michel Foucault, *The Use of Pleasure* (Pantheon, 1986), p. 12.
3. *The Foucault Reader,* ed. Paul Rabinow (Pantheon, 1984), p. 359.
4. Sigmund Freud, *The Interpretation of Dreams* (Avon, 1965), pp. 645–46, n. 2.
5. Michel Foucault, *Power/Knowledge,* ed. Colin Gordon (Pantheon, 1980), p. 220.
6. Foucault, *Foucault Live,* p. 102.
7. David Halperin, *One Hundred Years of Homosexuality* (Routledge, 1990), p. 6.
8. Foucault, *Foucault Live,* p. 205.
9. *Ibid.*, p. 204.
10. *Ibid.*, p. 207.
11. *Ibid.*, p. 205.
12. Foucault, *The Foucault Reader,* p. 350.
13. *Ibid.*, p. 351.
14. *Ibid.*, p. 335.

15. Michel Foucault, *Technologies of the Self*, eds. Luther H. Martin, Huck Gutman and Patrick H. Hutton (University of Massachusetts, 1988), p. 152.

16. Foucault, *The Foucault Reader*, p. 45.

17. Michel Foucault, "Michel Foucault on Attica," *Telos*, vol. 19 (1974), pp. 155–56.

18. Foucault, *Power/Knowledge*, pp. 223–24.

19. Michel Foucault, *The History of Sexuality* (Pantheon, 1980), p. 150.

20. Foucault, *The Foucault Reader*, p. 45.

21. Michel Foucault, "The Ethic of the Care for the Self as a Practice of Freedom," in *Philosophy and Social Criticism*, vols. 2–3 (Summer 1987), p. 131.

22. Foucault, *Foucault Live*, p. 313.

23. Michel Foucault, *L'impossible Prison* (Seuil, 1980), p. 46.

24. Michel Foucault, "Afterword," in H. Dreyfus and P. Rabinow, *Michel Foucault: Beyond Structuralism and Hermeneutics* (Chicago, 1982), p. 222.

25. Foucault, *The Foucault Reader*, p. 245.

26. Foucault, *The Foucault Reader*, p. 245.

27. Foucault, "The Ethic of the Care for the Self," p. 115.

28. Foucault, *The Foucault Reader*, p. 46.

29. Foucault, "The Ethic of the Care for the Self," pp. 113–14.

30. *Ibid.*, p. 114.

31. Foucault, *Foucault Live*, p. 311.

32. *Ibid.*

33. *Ibid.*

34. Foucault, "The Ethic of the Care for the Self," p. 116.

35. *Ibid.*, p. 117.

36. Foucault, *Technologies of the Self*, p. 153.

37. Foucault, "Afterword," p. 220.

38. Hannah Arendt, "What is Freedom?" in *Between Past and Future* (Viking, 1961), p. 145.

39. Arnaldo Momigliano, "Freedom of Speech in Antiquity" in *The Dictionary of the History of Ideas* (Scribners, 1973), pp. 252–63.

40. Foucault, *Foucault Live*, p. 314.

41. Michel Foucault, *The Use of Pleasure* (Random House, 1985), p. 9 (translation modified).

42. *Ibid.,* (translation modified).

43. Foucault, *L'impossible Prison,* p. 55.

44. *Ibid.,* p. 55.

45. Foucault, *Power/Knowledge,* p. 133.

46. Foucault, *L'impossible Prison,* p. 51.

47. Foucault, *The Foucault Reader,* p. 336.

48. Foucault, *Foucault Live,* p. 314.

49. Foucault, *Technologies of the Self,* p. 22.

50. Foucault, *Foucault Live,* p. 321.

51. Foucault, "The Ethic of the Care for the Self," p. 131.

52. Foucault, *The Foucault Reader,* p. 343.

53. Paul Veyne, "The Roman Empire," in *A History of Private Life* (Harvard, 1987).

54. Foucault, "Afterword," p. 210.

55. Foucault, *Language, Counter-memory, Practice,* p. 163.

56. Foucault, *Power/Knowledge,* p. 53.

57. Foucault, "Afterword," p. 210.

58. Foucault, *The Foucault Reader,* p. 386.

59. Foucault, *Foucault Live,* p. 308.

60. Foucault, "The Ethic of the Care for the Self," p. 125.

61. Foucault, *Language, Counter-memory, Practice,* pp. 202–203.

62. Foucault, *Foucault Live,* p. 324.

63. Foucault, *Language, Counter-memory, Practice,* p. 30.

64. Foucault, *The Use of Pleasure,* p. 8 (translation modified).

The Question of Ethics

1. Bernard Williams, "The Need to be Skeptical," *Times Literary Supplement* (Feb. 16–22, 1990), pp. 163–64.

Index

155